A COLLECTION OF
Indo-global recipes
BOOK 1 ENTREES & SIDES

BY IRA GHOSH

NewDelhi • London

BLUEROSE PUBLISHERS
India | U.K.

Copyright © Ira Ghosh 2025

All rights reserved by author. No part of this publication may be reproduced, stored in a retrieval system or transmitted in any form or by any means, electronic, mechanical, photocopying, recording or otherwise, without the prior permission of the author. Although every precaution has been taken to verify the accuracy of the information contained herein, the publisher assumes no responsibility for any errors or omissions. No liability is assumed for damages that may result from the use of information contained within.

BlueRose Publishers takes no responsibility for any damages, losses, or liabilities that may arise from the use or misuse of the information, products, or services provided in this publication.

For permissions requests or inquiries regarding this publication, please contact:

BLUEROSE PUBLISHERS
www.BlueRoseONE.com
info@bluerosepublishers.com
+91 8882 898 898
+4407342408967

ISBN: 978-93-6452-275-5

Cover design: Yash Singhal
Typesetting: Namrata Saini

First Edition: January 2025

DEDICATION

I dedicate this book to my late husband Ashis Bindu Ghosh. When we married, I could barely cook! However, my culinary abilities grew and flourished through his constant encouragement and support (and unfailing good humour at some of my less successful creations). His career enabled us to live in different countries and experience and appreciate different cultures. Much later, after I had accumulated my varied collection of recipes from around the world, he encouraged me to share them through their publication. He was instrumental in getting the first version of my recipe collection into a publishable form. If it were not for his hard work, support, and encouragement, this book would not exist, and I would not have been able to share my recipe collection with you.

I also dedicate this book to my mother Ratnavali Baruah who was a very good cook and had some fantastic recipes. She however, never had any set formula. Before my marriage my mother always worried about my lack of culinary ability!

Additionally, I dedicate this book to my grandmother Pragna Sundari Devi who was the first person to author a series of systematic cookbooks in Bengali extending to several volumes. Her books were my constant reference abroad, from which I learnt my basics.

TABLE OF CONTENTS

Introduction 1
Weights, Measures, & Temperatures 3

VEGETABLES 7

    Simple Fried Spinach 9
    Garlic & Lemon Carrots 10
    Lemon Mint Carrots 11
    Lemon Broccoli 12
    Lemon Green Papaya 13
    Sara's Papaya Tarkari (Curried Green Papaya) 14
    Sara's Egg Plant 15
    Indian Summer Vegetables 16
    Aginares Á La Polita 17
    Braised Aubergine Or Cucumber 18
    Methi Aloo (Potatoes With Fenugreek Greens) 19
    Indian Summer Vegetables As Accompaniment 20
    Baked Zucchini 22
    Hasselbacks – Swedish Baked Potato 23
    Baked "Lau" Or "Lauki" (White Gourd) With Cheese 24
    Baked Potato – Finnish Style 25
    Karjalan Pirakat 26
    Banana Flower (Mowcha) Pizza Or Pie 27
    Spinach, Tomato & Cottage Cheese Pie 28
    Savoury Paneer (Cottage Cheese) Pie 29
    Potato Pancakes In The Oven 30
    Bean Curd 31
    Tomato Eggs 32
    Mowcha (Banana Flower) Kebab 33
    Green Jackfruit Burgers 34
    Armenian Stuffed Cabbage 35
    Swiss Chard Salad 36
    Bread Salad 37
    Simple Tomato Salad 38

Taboulé 39

Rudjak Genit – Indonesian Salad 40

Melezana (Greek Aubergine Salad)...41

German Farmer's Salad 42

Apple Salad 43

Green Papaya Salad 44

Chola/Chana (Chickpea or Garbanzo Bean) Salad...........................45

Indian Salad 46

Spinach & Potato Salad..47

Curried Pasta Salad..48

FISH & SEAFOOD..49

Grilled Fish 51

Mock Grilled Fish...53

Fish Pie 54

Bar-B-Q Whole Fish with Coconut Sauce 55

Simple Baked Fish 56

Baked Tomato Fish 57

Guyanese Baked Fish in Wine..58

Guyanese Baked Fish Supreme 59

Fish Chops - Economical..60

Bengali Fish Chop 61

Curried Fish Cakes...63

Fish Roll 64

Masala Or Spicy Pomfret..66

Malaysian Stuffed Fish 67

Tangy Fish..68

Lemon Garlic Butter Fish...69

Fish In Garlic & Tomato Sauce 70

Fish & Mushroom In Wine Sauce 72

Fish In Oriental White Sauce...73

Anchovy Roll..74

Potato Chops With Roe Filling 76

Roe Pudding...77

Lemon Fish...78

Smothered Lobster Or Crayfish Meat 79

Seafood Creole Style 80
Hungarian Fish (Rāc) 81
Chinese Fish 82
Fish In Black Bean Sauce 83
Lobster In Wine Sauce 84
Malaysian Sweet & Sour Prawns Or Lobsters (Mesah Pedas) 85
Garlic & Chilli Prawn 86
Sweet & Sour Prawn Balls 87
Crab Casserole 88
Stuffed Crab 89
Baked Crab 90
Fish Brown Stew 91
Fish White Stew 92
Stellamashi's Hilsa Pārā (Pickled Hilsa) 93
Smoked Hilsa - The Easy Way 94
Cold Herring Swedish Style 95
Fried Prawns 96
Tempura (I) 97
Tempura (Ii) 99
Mummy's Masala (Or Spicy) Fish 100
Stuffed Fish 102

POULTRY 103

Chicken With Oranges 105
Curried Orange Chicken 106
Tomato Chicken 107
Quick Spicy Chicken 109
Piquant Chicken 111
Chicken With Sweet Hot Sauce 112
Chicken Cognac 113
Cheesy Chicken With Sour Cream 114
Piquant Chicken Stew 116
Groundnut Stew 117
Savoury Cake With Chicken Filling 119
Stuffed Roast Chicken 120
Chicken & Corn Bake (I) 121

Chicken & Corn Bake (II) 122
Chicken & Asparagus 123
Baked Chicken 124
Chicken Baked With Garlic 125
Italian Flavoured Baked Chicken 126
Baked Cubed Chicken Breasts 127
Chicken Pancakes Au Gratin 128
Grilled Chicken 130
Bar-B-q'ed Or Grilled Chicken Tengri (Leg) 131
Yakitori – Chicken Sheesh Kebab Japanese Style 132
Crumb Fried Chicken Cutlets 133
Black Pepper Chicken Fry 134
Quick Chicken Stir Fry 135
Chicken Fried In Cheese Batter 136
Chinese Fried Chicken 137
Chilli Chicken 138
Fried Chicken A La Muslim 139
Chicken Muslim Style 141
Chopped Chicken Liver 142
Creamed Chicken And Noodle 143
Noky (Noodles) With Chicken Sauce – Czech Style 144
Kowshwe 146
Fried Duck With Thick Spicy Gravy 148
Mummy's Duck Haari ('Cooking Pot') Kabab 149

LAMB & MUTTON 151

Lamb Chops 153
Breaded Lamb Chops 154
Lamb Chops Casserole 155
Lamb Casserole 156
Stewed Lamb Chops 157
Kashmiri Mutton Chops 158
Saté Kambing – Indonesian Sheesh Kebab 159
Armenian Sheesh Kebab 160
Shami Kebab (I) 161
Shami Kebab (II) 162

Hamburger Cutlets 163
Cheese & Pineapple Hamburger.. 164
Battered Meat 165
Youvourlakia Or Undressed Dolmas 166
Closed Lahmedjun (Armenian) 168
Moussaka 169
Crepé A La Rognon 171
Steamed Liver The Chinese Way 172

BEEF 173

Ground Beef & Baked Beans 175
Beef'n Beans 176
Veal Loaf 177
Beef Casserole 178
Crusty Beef Pie 179
Beef And Ginger Rice 181
Beef Rolls 182
Cabbage Dolmas 183
Osang Osang Beans (Indonesian) 184
Oven Meat Balls 185
Meat Balls With Fettucine 186
Sweet & Sour Balls With Lo-Mein 187
Meat Balls In Cheese Sauce 189
Meat Balls In Wine Sauce 190
Meat Balls In Tomato Sauce With Noodles 191
Teriyaki Burgers 193
Easy Barbecued Hamburgers 194
Hamburgers (II) 195
Hungarian Goulash (I) 196
Hungarian Goulash (II) 197
Simple Beaf Steak 198
Barbecued Or Grilled Steak 199
Simple Pepper Steak (I) 200
Pepper Steak (II) 201
Steak & Kidney Galantine 202
Oven Baked Or Pressure-Cooked Leg Of Beef 203

Cheesy Veal Escalopes 204

Stuffed Veal Escalopes Or Beef Fillet Slices 205

Salted Beef 207

Pressed Beef Tongue 208

Sudanese Tongue 209

PORK 211

Oriental Pork Chops 213

Cheesy Pork Chops 214

Tasty Pork Chops 215

Sweet & Sour Pork Balls With Pineapple 216

Pork Balls Swedish Style 217

Sliced Pork & Noodles With Peanut Sauce 218

Pork With Sauerkrat 219

Swedish Cabbage Dolmas 220

Sweet & Sour Pork 221

Oven Fried Pork Ribs 222

Yakinoko Or Japanese Barbecued Pork 223

Tan Chun (Chinese Sliced Pancakes) 224

Filled Ham Rolls 225

Ham, Eggs & Tomato Pie 226

Stella Mashi's Salted Pork 228

Glossary 230

Alphabetical List of Recipes 235

INTRODUCTION

"*A Collection of Indo Global Recipes*", as the name suggests, is a collection of recipes that is influenced by my Indian background, as well as being the result of spending many years in different countries where my husband's job took me. While abroad, I actively participated in various international groups and made friends with people from many different countries.

I do not consider myself a great cook! However, I was always interested in collecting and devising new recipes and trying them out on friends and family. Their enthusiastic responses indicated that I must have been doing something right! Hoping that others might wish to enjoy the pleasure of cooking and experimenting with recipes from around the world with minimum effort, I decided to publish my collection. In addition to many of the Indian recipes I inherited or learned from my family, I have been building this collection since my husband's first international posting in 1967. I have also added to the collection recipes that I invented over this time. I have tried out all the recipes, and this book is the result of my explorations, collection, and experimentation. Many of the recipes have familiar names, but often prepared differently by various cooks. I tried to simplify each recipe, and in doing so built up a collection that is user-friendly. In a few recipes I could not forgo the temptation of using "ajinomoto" (MSG; monosodium glutamate) as this was a popular ingredient when I collected the recipes. In the intervening years, it was reputed to be harmful, but recently it has been classified by the U.S. Food and Drug Administration of being safe. However, if there is concern, ajinomoto may be replaced with a pinch of sugar to retain somewhat similar flavour.

I hope my work will be of use to many enthusiastic and curious cooks including the offspring of Indian diaspora living abroad, youthful techies wishing to serve party-fares, connoisseurs researching ethnic cooking, and adventurous cooks wanting to make good, interesting food with ease from diverse recipes. Some of the dishes remain time-consuming, but most can be made with a few quick and easy steps.

This book was a labour of love, and my family encouraged me through the years I took to complete this project. I published the first version of this collection, entitled "*A Collection of Recipes*" in 2012 in one large volume. My husband did the tremendous job of computerization and editing that version. However, before I could publish my book, I needed to first complete another important project. I had taken on the colossal task of editing the multi-volume cookbook in Bengali titled "*Amish O Niramish Ahar*" written by my grandmother Pragna Sundari Devi. My grandmother was the first writer of a systematic cookbook in Bengali. Her volumes were published starting from the year 1900 AD. My re-edited and re-arranged versions were published in 1995, after which I could concentrate on my recipe collection. In the years since I first published my collection, I have received feedback and added to it. It is now timely to re-edit and publish the current collection, but this time as a four-volume set to make it more accessible, user friendly, and with a slight change in title to reflect its roots in both Indian and international cuisines. My son, Dr. Richik Niloy Ghosh, was instrumental in helping me create this new four-volume version.

Many thanks are due to my relations and friends in India and abroad from whom I collected the original recipes, modified versions of which now appear in these pages. I am unable to thank them all individually. As my sources were from many nationalities using various units of measurements (metric, avoirdupois, and cups), I kept the units as were given in the originals. To assist the users, I have appended a conversion table covering the three systems. A glossary has also been added to help the reader to understand unfamiliar terms.

Bon Appétit

Ira Ghosh

29 February 2024

WEIGHTS, MEASURES, & TEMPERATURES

1. SOLID MEASURES

1 kg. (kilogram) = 1,000 gm. (gram) = 2.2 lb. (pound avoirdupois)

1 lb. = 16 oz. (ounce)

(a) Equivalent measures of some commodities

Avoirdupois measure	Commodity	Container equivalent
1 pound	Butter or other fat	2 cups
1 pound	Flour	4 cups
1 pound	Granulated or castor sugar	2 cups
1 pound	Icing or confectioner's sugar	3 cups
1 pound	Brown (moist) sugar	2 cups
1 pound	Golden syrup or treacle	1 cup
1 pound	Rice	2 cups
1 pound	Dried fruit	2 cups
1 pound	Chopped meat (finely packed)	2 cups
1 pound	Lentils or split peas	2 cups
1 pound	Coffee (beans)	2 cups
1 pound	Soft breadcrumbs	4 cups
½ ounce	Flour	1 level tablespoon
1 ounce	Flour	1 heaped tablespoon
1 ounce	Sugar	1 level tablespoon
¾ ounce	Butter	1 tablespoon smoothed off
1 ounce	Golden syrup or treacle	1 tablespoon
1 ounce	Jam or jelly	1 level tablespoon

(b) Dry volume/ weight measures

Container	Container	Volume	Weight
4 teaspoons (tsp.)	1 tablespoon	½ fluid ounce	14.3 grams
2 tablespoons (tblsp.)	⅛ cup	1 fluid ounce	28.6 grams
4 tablespoons	⅓ cup	2 fluid ounces	56.7 grams
5⅓ tablespoons	½ cup	2.6 fluid ounce	75.6 grams
8 tablespoons	½ cup	4 fluid ounces	113.4 grams
12 tablespoons	¾ cup	6 fluid ounces	170 grams (.375 pound)
32 tablespoons	2 cups	16 fluid ounces	453.6 grams (1 Pound)
64 tablespoons	4 cups	32 fluid ounces	907 grams (2 pounds)

2. LIQUID MEASURES

(a) Common usage

Measure	Measure	Measure	Volume
1 cup	8 fluid ounces	½ pint	237 millilitres
2 cups	16 fluid ounces	1 pint	474 millilitres.
4 cups	32 fluid ounces	1 quart	946 millilitres
1 pint	16 fluid ounces	½ quart	473 millilitres
2 pints	32 fluid ounces	1 quart	0.964 litres.
4 quarts	128 fluid ounces	1 gallon	3.784 litres
8 quarts	One peck		
4 pecks	One bushel		
dash	Less than ¼ teaspoon		

(b) Small quantities

1 teaspoon (US)	1/6 ounce	4.93 millilitres
1 tablespoon (US)	0.5 ounce	3 teaspoons
1 teaspoon (UK)	1.2 teaspoon (US)	6.16 millilitres
1 tablespoon (UK)	1.2 tablespoon (US)	18.48 millilitres
1 dessert spoon (UK)	2.4 teaspoons	12.32 millilitres
1 dash	~ ⅛ teaspoon	~ 0.6 millilitres

3. APPROXIMATE OVEN TEMPERATURES

Oven	Gas Regulo	Electricity	
		°F	°C
Cool	0 - ½	225 – 250	107 – 121
Very Slow	½ - 1	250 – 275	121 -135
Slow	1 - 2	275 – 300	135 – 149
Very Moderate	2 – 3	300 – 350	149 – 177
Moderate	4	375	190
Moderately Hot	5	400	204
Hot	6 – 7	435 – 450	218 – 233
Very Hot	8 - 9	475 - 500	245 - 260

Ovens might somewhat differ in their specifications.

VEGETABLES

SIMPLE FRIED SPINACH

2 tblsp. oil	1 dry chilli
¼ tsp. whole mustard seeds	500 gm. spinach washed and roughly chopped
¼ cup warm water	Salt to taste

Method

Heat oil. Add chilli and mustard seeds. When they begin to splutter add the spinach and stir. Add water, salt, and cover. Cook for 7-10 minutes.

Be careful when adding salt as spinach is naturally salty. To get the salty and bitter flavour out, soak spinach after washing, in a solution of water and a little sodium bicarbonate for a few minutes. Rinse well and then chop.

Variation:

With the dry chilli and whole mustard seeds also add 2-3 cloves of garlic.

GARLIC & LEMON CARROTS

250 gm. medium carrots cut lengthwise or, whole baby carrots

½-1 tsp. (or more) garlic powder

Salt and pepper to taste

1 tblsp. lemon juice

2 tsp. olive oil

½-1 tsp. 'chaat masala'

¼-½ tsp. paprika

½-1 tsp. dried parsley/mint/basil/thyme crumbled

½ tsp. lemon zest

Method

Steam the carrots. In a non-stick pan, sauté the carrots in the oil with the spices, seasonings, and herbs for 1-2 minutes. Add the lemon juice and zest. Stir to mix. Serve as an accompaniment to any main course.

LEMON MINT CARROTS

2 large carrots sliced in thin rounds

Salt and pepper to taste

2 tblsp. white vinegar or, fresh lemon juice

2 tblsp. fresh mint leaves finely chopped or, 1 tblsp. dried mint

Method

Steam carrot slices. Drain all liquid. Cool. Add the vinegar/lemon juice, salt & pepper. Toss in the mint and mix well. Serve as an accompaniment to any main course.

LEMON BROCCOLI

250-300 gm. broccoli separated in florets

1 tblsp. (more or less) lemon juice

Salt and pepper to taste

½-1 tsp. olive oil

½-1 tsp. lemon zest

Method

Stir fry broccoli in oil for 1-2 minutes. Add lemon juice, salt, and pepper. Stir to mix. Take off heat. Sprinkle zest and toss to coat the broccoli.

LEMON GREEN PAPAYA

500 gm. green papaya

Salt and pepper to taste

2-4 tblsp. fresh lime juice

¼ tsp. paprika (optional)

Method

Remove skin and seeds, if any, of papaya. Boil and mash fine. Add lemon juice and seasoning. Mix well. A good accompaniment with any meat or fish dish.

Variation: 1-2 tblsp melted butter may also be added if desired.

SARA'S PAPAYA TARKARI (CURRIED GREEN PAPAYA)

1-2 tsp. oil	500 gm. green papaya steamed and mashed
1 tsp. fresh roasted & ground coriander	1 tsp. fresh roasted & ground cumin
1 tsp. 'amchoor' (mango powder)	1 tsp. curry powder/'chaat masala' (optional)
Salt to taste	1-2 tsp. turmeric powder
4 tblsp. (or more) lemon juice	2-3 whole green chillis split and de-seeded

Method

In very little oil sauté the papaya for a few minutes and then add all the spice powders and chilli. Stir a couple of times and then take off heat. Cool and add plenty of lime juice and serve as an accompaniment to a main course with other curries.

Variation: The papaya need not be sautéed. Instead mix in all the spices and green chillis to the mash and then add the lemon juice.

SARA'S EGG PLANT

2-3 large egg plants	1 or 2 tblsp. oil
2-4 tblsp. ground onion	1-2 tsp. ground ginger
½-1 tsp. garlic powder or, crushed	1-2 tsp. cumin powder
1-2 tsp. coriander powder	½-1 tsp. turmeric powder
Salt to taste	½-1 tblsp. yogurt/tomato purée (optional)
1-2 fresh green chillis de-seeded and chopped	1-2 tblsp. fresh coriander leaves chopped

Method

Cut egg plants in half. Next scrape all the pulp out of the egg plant halves without damaging the skin at the base. Heat oil and cook the pulp after mashing roughly with all the above ingredients like a curry. Just before taking off heat add the chopped coriander leaves reserving a few for the garnish. Put the filling back into the halved egg plants very sparingly. Join the halves by pressing down lightly with the palms. Rub all over generously with oil. Barbecue the egg plants or place under the grill. Turn from time to time to cook evenly. Take off heat when soft and cooked. Serve garnished with parsley. Alternately, pack the halves with the filling, drizzle tops with oil generously and then place under the grill till soft and cooked. Garnish tops with coriander leaves before serving. If desired the filling can be taken out of the plants and served with a garnish of coriander leaves, chopped onions and chillis.

INDIAN SUMMER VEGETABLES

6 long green Indian summer beans (borboti) chopped fine

2 tsp. oil

1 tsp. soy sauce

½" fresh ginger sliced thin

1 tblsp. fresh/dried basil chopped/crumbled

A pinch of sugar or MSG

1 medium green pepper de-seeded and chopped small

2 small eggplants cubed

1 large soft tomato chopped

1 fresh green chilli de-seeded and chopped

½ cup water or, as required

Salt to taste

Method

Sauté beans, eggplants, and green pepper in oil till soft. Next add the soya sauce, tomatoes, ginger, green chilli, basil, and water and keep cooking over moderate heat till mushy. Add salt, sugar stir. Take off heat and serve cooled as an accompaniment with any meat, poultry, or fish dish.

Note: 2-4 tblsp. ketchup or tomato puree can be substituted in place of fresh tomatoes.

AGINARES Á LA POLITA

1½-2 kg. (approx. 14) artichokes

3 cups water

2 medium onions chopped

2-3 carrots cut in thin rounds/slices

1 tblsp. fresh dill leaves chopped

½-1 cup olive oil

1-1½ cup lemon juice

1 tblsp. flour

2-3 spring onions chopped

2-3 potatoes (optional)

Salt and pepper to taste

Method

Only use the heart of the artichoke. Clean and cut in half if too big. Immediately soak in a mixture of lemon juice, water, and flour to keep the artichoke white. Put onions, spring onions, carrots, artichokes, potatoes, dill, salt, and pepper. Pour sufficient olive oil over the vegetables. Now pour the lemon juice, water and flour mixed well, over all. Cover the pan with a sheet of grease-proof paper with a small hole in the centre. Cover tightly with the lid. Simmer on low heat for about 1 hour. Alternately microwave on low for 2 minutes to ½ hour or till done.

BRAISED AUBERGINE OR CUCUMBER

1 tblsp. oil

1 large onion sliced thickly

1 tblsp. garlic and chilli sauce

2 tsp. soya sauce

4 large, long aubergines/cucumbers each cut in eight pieces

2 tsp. tomato purée or ketchup

¼ cup or less water

½ tsp. green chilli powder or, 1 small green chilli de-seeded and sliced

Method

Heat oil slightly and sauté the vegetables and onion till soft. Mix all the sauces with the water in a bowl and pour over the vegetables. Cook for a few more minutes till gravy thickens. Add the green chilli powder or de-seeded and chopped green chilli just before taking off the heat. For sautéed cucumber chopped dill leaves may be used in which case, omit the garlic, and use plain chilli sauce.

METHI ALOO (POTATOES WITH FENUGREEK GREENS)

8 bunches or more fresh fenugreek greens	1 tblsp. oil
1-2 dry red chillis	1 kg. potatoes cut into small cubes
1 tsp. fenugreek seeds	Salt to taste

Method

Cut potatoes into very small cubes. Wash and clean the fenugreek greens thoroughly and then chop coarsely. Heat oil slightly. Add the fenugreek seeds and chilli. When they begin to splutter add the potato cubes, salt and fry stirring frequently till they are almost done. Add the greens and stir fry with the potatoes till well mixed and done. This can be served with any dish as an accompaniment or with any Indian bread.

INDIAN SUMMER VEGETABLES AS ACCOMPANIMENTS

(I) Aubergine

1. Purée or Mash

Dry roast 1 large aubergine on a griddle, under the grill or in a hot oven turning frequently. Peel off the outer burnt skin and mash the pulp with a fork till smooth. Alternately purée in a food-processor. Add 1 tsp (or according to taste) garlic powder, 2 tblsp. olive oil, 1 tblsp lemon juice or wine vinegar, ½ tsp mustard powder, salt & pepper to taste. If desired a pinch of cayenne or paprika may be added. Grease a bowl and then pack it with the mash smoothening out the top. Leave for 5-10 minutes and then invert on to a flat dish. Garnish with a few fresh parsley or mint leaves.

Alternatively, put in a food processor.

2. Batter fried

Make a fritter batter. Dip thickly sliced aubergine in the batter and either deep fry or shallow fry in a non-stick pan. Drain on paper towels before serving.

Alternately, make a thick batter with chick-pea flour (besan) and water. Any of the following could be added to the batter according to the taste – ajowan (ptychotis), crushed black pepper, paprika, minced green chilli etc. etc. Rest for ½--1 hour. Dip aubergine slices and proceed as above.

3. Sautéed

Cook 500 gms thick aubergine slices with 2-3 sliced onions in a non-stick pan with very little oil. Until soft and golden brown. In a bowl mix ½ cup water, 1 tblsp ketchup, ½ tblsp. soya sauce, Worcester sauce or any other sauce of choice. Add to the aubergine. Continue cooking till thick. (The aubergine can be sliced in rounds or lengthwise.) The slices should remain whole and not become mushy. If desired, 1 medium de-seeded green pepper thinly sliced may be added during the last few minutes of cooking.

(II) Green Papaya

1. Cold Purée or Mash

Steam or pressure cook green papaya cut roughly. Drain water and purée. Mix lemon juice or wine vinegar and salt & pepper all to taste. Mold and un-mold like aubergine mash and serve cold.

Alternately, the papaya purée can be served mixed with mayonnaise or a French dressing. Garnish with parsley or mint leaves chopped.

2. Sautéed

Cook as in "Sautéed Aubergine"

(III) Red Pumpkin

Follow all three versions of the "Green Papaya" recipes.

(IV) Lady's Fingers or Okra

Cut each Okra in half or in very thin slices. Dust with salt and pepper and fry crisp or just sauté in very little oil in a non-stick pan.

Alternately, cut Okra in small rounds. Heat a little oil in a nonstick frying pan. Add a few black onion seeds (Kala Jeera or Kalonji)) on medium heat. When they start to splutter add the okra. Cook till soft and done.

Alternately, sauté the okra slices with sliced onions and then add tomato purée mixed with a little water. Add salt & pepper to taste along with a little paprika if desired. Cook for a few more minutes and serve hot.

BAKED ZUCCHINI

2 lb. zucchini peeled and thinly sliced

1 small onion minced

1 can (8-12 oz. approx.) mushroom soup

Salt and pepper to taste

¼ tsp. or more paprika

3 tblsp. butter

3 tblsp. flour

½ cup white wine

Grated parmesan cheese for sprinkling

Method

Boil zucchini in salted water for 10 minutes. Drain and place in a greased baking dish. Cook butter and onion in a saucepan for about 5 minutes. Blend in flour. Next add the soup and wine. Keep stirring with a wooden spoon till thick. Add seasoning. Pour sauce over zucchini. Sprinkle with parmesan and paprika. Bake in a moderate or moderately hot oven for about 25 minutes. (350°–375° F).

Variations: Chicken breast sliced or legs, Pork slices or chops, squash or cucumber slices or diced, may be cooked in this way also.

HASSELBACKS – SWEDISH BAKED POTATO

6 potatoes

3-4 tblsp. butter

Salt to taste

4-6 tblsp. parmesan or cheddar cheese grated

Method

Peel the potatoes and cut into thin slices very close together like garlic bread without cutting right through. Brush potatoes well with melted butter and salt. Bake in med. low oven for 1 ½ - 2 hours or till done. Keep brushing with butter from time to time during cooking. Just before they are ready sprinkle generously with cheese Serve hot as an accompaniment to any meat dish. Parmesan is preferable to cheddar. To cut down on the cooking time boil the potatoes for 10 minutes, cool and then proceed as above.

BAKED "LAU" OR "LAUKI" (WHITE GOURD) WITH CHEESE

(2 kg gourd steamed, drained of all water, and mashed – preferably in a pressure cooker for 5 minutes or Icmic cooker for 10 minutes. If neither of the two latter items available, the gourd may be steamed in the traditional method.)

White Sauce:

3 tblsp. butter	1 large onion chopped
2 tblsp. flour or, corn flour	½ pt. milk
2-3 egg yolks	2 tblsp. any cheese grated
1 tsp. chives chopped	1 bunch spring onions chopped finely
1 small capsicum deseeded and chopped fine	2-3 egg whites
Salt and pepper to taste	1-2 tblsp. breadcrumbs
1-2 tblsp. parmesan cheese grated	Salt and pepper to taste

Method

In a heavy bottom saucepan place 2 tblsp. butter, onion and flour. Stir over low heat stirring continuously with a wooden spoon till the butter melts and all the ingredients are well blended. Do not let the mixture burn or stick to the bottom of the pan. Now pour the milk into the mixture very slowly stirring continuously till it begins to thicken. Take off heat. Add yolks one at a time blending with a wooden spoon after each addition. Next add the cheese, again mixing to blend well with a wooden spoon. Last of all add the gourd, chives, spring onions, capsicum, salt, and pepper and stir till all well mixed. Beat the egg whites till stiff. Gently fold into the gourd mixture. Pour into a buttered oven proof dish. Cover top with parmesan and breadcrumbs. Bake in a moderate oven for 15 –20 minutes or microwave on power 7 for about 5 minutes or till top is brown. A good accompaniment with any meat, chicken dish.

BAKED POTATO – FINNISH STYLE

2 kg. potatoes boiled, peeled, and mashed

2 tblsp. sugar

2 tblsp. butter

2 tblsp. flour

2 tsp. salt

½ litre milk

Method

Mix the mashed potatoes with the flour, sugar, salt, butter, and milk. Cover with a tea towel and let it rest for 2-3 hrs or more. Stir, place in a baking dish, and bake in a low warm oven for several hrs or till a nice golden-brown colour. Serve with any meat dish.

KARJALAN PIRAKAT

(Karjalia is a province of Finland)

Dough:

100 gm. wheat flour	200 gm. rye flour or, atta
1¾ cup (approx.) water	1 tsp. salt

Filling:

1½ cups rice	1 tblsp. butter
1 litre milk	

Method

Cook all the filling ingredients together till the liquid is all absorbed. Keep aside till the dough is ready. Now mix all the dry dough ingredients together. Add sufficient water to make a pliable dough. Make the dough into an oval pie shape. Place the filling in the centre lengthwise. Form the pastry into the shape of a boat. Lift and place carefully on a baking sheet or tray. Bake in a medium oven for about 10–15 minutes. The pastry should be hard but not brown. If pastry is to be used later then dip the boat in about 2 cups milk and 100 gm. melted butter. Cover with foil/ cling wrap/grease proof paper and freeze till required. Take out and heat before serving. Serve with chopped eggs sprinkled with salt and butter. Rice filling can be substituted with mashed potatoes. This can be served as an entrée, first course or tea-time/cocktail snack.

BANANA FLOWER (MOWCHA) PIZZA OR PIE

Method

Line a pie pan with either short crust pastry or pizza dough. Line the bottom of the pastry/dough with a thin layer of cottage cheese mixed with ketchup. Cover with any left-over "mowcha ghonto" (see under "Curries" in this book.). Bake in a hot oven for 15-20 minutes or till ready. Delicious eating!

Note: Any other dry or mushy vegetable curry can be substituted.

SPINACH, TOMATO & COTTAGE CHEESE PIE

Short crust pastry with 8 oz. flour
Salt, freshly ground pepper, and chilli powder to taste
2 lb. spinach cooked and puréed
8 oz. cottage cheese sliced or crumbled

2-4. oz. fresh breadcrumbs
1-2 tblsp. butter/cream

8 oz. tomatoes chopped
1-2 tsp. Worcester sauce

Method

Line a pie tin with the pastry. Sprinkle the base with a handful of breadcrumbs. Place in a hot oven for about 10 minutes or till half baked. In the meantime, mix the seasonings, sauce, butter/cream with the spinach. Fill pastry with the spinach mixture evenly. Spread the chopped tomatoes on top. Last of all, cover with the cottage cheese. Sprinkle top lightly with a handful of breadcrumbs. Bake in a moderate oven for 10–15 minutes or till done. The breadcrumbs should be of an even golden-brown colour. Slice and serve either as an accompaniment to a main course or by itself.

SAVOURY PANEER (COTTAGE CHEESE) PIE

Short Crust Pastry:

8 oz. flour sifted	1 tsp. salt
2 oz. butter/margarine	2 oz. Crisco/vanaspati (hydrogenated oil)

Filling:

1-2 eggs	2 cups paneer (cottage cheese)
Sufficient milk or fresh cream (2-4 tblsp.) to moisten filling	2-3 slices bacon minus fat (optional) or, 6-8 mushrooms chopped and sautéed
1-2 tomatoes chopped (optional)	Salt and pepper to taste
½ tsp. paprika (optional)	

Method

Make the pastry by mixing all the dry ingredients together. Add the two types of fat and stir with wooden spoon till mixture resembles breadcrumbs. Add enough cold (refrigerated) water to bind dough. It should not be too dry or too sticky. Form into a ball, cover with a cloth and refrigerate till required.

Now mix all the filling ingredients. Add enough milk/cream to moisten filling. Spread some dry flour on the work surface. Roll out dough into a round about ¼"thick. Gently lift and line a greased and floured medium (6-8") flan/pie tin evenly. Spread base of pie with breadcrumbs. Pile the filling into the pastry case and smoothen out top with a spatula or the back of a knife. Bake in a hot oven for about ½ hour or till pie is done.

POTATO PANCAKES IN THE OVEN

2 tblsp. flour
Salt and pepper to taste
1 medium onion chopped

Milk (optional)
1 egg (optional)

¼ tsp. baking soda (optional)
2 tblsp. cheddar cheese grated
250 gm. potatoes – raw grated/boiled mashed
Oil as required

Method

Sift the dry ingredients together. Add the rest of the ingredients and mix well. Add the milk, if required only if the mixture is too dry. Grease a baking tray and drop mixture on it in spoonfuls with a medium rounded soup spoon leaving enough space between each pancake. Flatten tops with a fork or back of a spoon slightly. Sprinkle tops with a generous amount of oil. Bake in a moderately hot oven for 10–15 minutes or till tops are an even golden brown. Serve hot as an accompaniment with any grilled/fried meat or fish dish or as a snack.

Variation: The pancakes can also be microwaved or cooked over direct heat. Grease a non-stick fry pan or griddle with 1-2 tblsp. oil. Drop pancakes in rounds. Flatten tops as above. No need to sprinkle oil on top. When one side is done turn over and cook the other side till golden brown. These can be cooked in batches.

BEAN CURD

(A lot of Chinese and other recipes need bean curd which is delicious to eat but often not easy to acquire. So, why not make your own bean curd which is not difficult to make. It also has an added advantage – it can be stored in the refrigerator longer.)

1 kg. soybeans or, any other white or yellow beans

2 litres water (approximately)

2 tblsp China grass (agar or agar-agar)

Method

Soak beans for a few minutes in very little water (just enough to cover). When slightly soft, rub beans between the palms to take out the outer skin which should be discarded. Now put the beans with the water in the food processor to make a paste. Put the paste with water in a saucepan and boil for 20-30 minute Take off heat and add the China grass to set the bean curd. The bean curd mixed with the China grass should sink to the bottom of the pan. Strain off all water. Put the bean curd in between fine muslin or cheese cloth and place on a flat board, tray, or plate. Press down with another board to squeeze out all the moisture. When set and dry, remove the cloth and cut in cubes. Soak in cold water for another 15-minutes. Store in refrigerator and use as and when needed.

TOMATO EGGS

3 tblsp. oil

½ tsp. each cumin & coriander powder

2 tsp. salt or, to taste

1-2 tblsp. vinegar

6-8 eggs (1 egg per person)

1-2 green chillis finely chopped (optional)

250 gm. onion chopped

½-1 tsp. chilli powder

2½ cups ripe red tomatoes chopped

1 tblsp. fresh coriander or, parsley leaves chopped

4-6 tsp. sugar

Method

Heat oil in a large fry pan. Add onions and fry till golden. Add cumin, coriander, chilli powder and salt and stir well. Keep frying till cooked. Add the tomatoes and mix well. Add green chillis and coriander/ parsley and keep on stirring till most of the liquid has evaporated. It should be thick. Add vinegar and sugar to get a sweet and sour taste. Again, stir and mix all well. Take off heat. This can be made a day before. Before serving grease with butter or margarine a slightly raised heat proof dish. Spread the tomato pulp evenly on it. Make as many hollows with a spoon as the number of eggs used. Break an egg in each hollow. Place dish covered on low heat until the eggs are done.

Alternately the dish may be put in a moderately low oven. Again, it can be placed in the microwave on high for 1 minute. or till the eggs are set. This should be made in a dish that can be placed at the dining table.

MOWCHA (BANANA FLOWER) KEBAB

1 large mowcha (300-500 gm.) cleaned and boiled	½ the quantity (150-250 gm.) soybean granules soaked for 1-2 hours
¼ cup more or less oil	2 large onions sliced thinly
1 tblsp. onion paste	1 tblsp. ginger paste
2 tsp. each coriander and cumin powder	Salt to taste
1-2 fresh chillis minced (optional)	2 tblsp. dry flour

Method

Chop the mowcha. Squeeze the water out of the soy granules. Mix and cook in 2 tsp oil with the onions and all the other spices till well browned and there is a nice aroma. Add the salt, green chillis and a little water only if necessary. Cool mixture and put in the grinder or food processor to form a smooth fairly dry paste. Form into kebabs. Roll in dry flour and shallow fry in a non-stick pan or griddle. Serve garnished with rings of raw onions and lemon wedges with a cucumber or tomato salad.

Variation: Add minced capsicum instead of green chillis and finely chopped spring onions to the paste before forming into kebabs.

GREEN JACKFRUIT BURGERS

4-6 tblsp. oil	500 gm. green jackfruit shredded
2 large onions sliced thin	2 tblsp. onion paste
1 tblsp. ginger paste	1 tblsp. garlic paste
1 tsp. turmeric powder (optional)	1 tsp coriander powder
1 tsp. cumin powder	Salt to taste
½ tsp. chilli powder or, paprika (optional)	4 tblsp. yogurt
1 tblsp. ketchup or, tomato paste	2 tblsp. dry flour

Method

Heat 1 tblsp oil. Fry jackfruit and onion slices together till brown. Add all the other spices and keep frying for 5-10 minutes on medium heat. Add salt and chilli powder if using. Stir and then add the yogurt and ketchup. If using tomato paste add a pinch of sugar. Stir well to mix and continue cooking till dry and mushy. Take off heat and cool. Put in the food processor to get a smooth mixture. Form into hamburger patties. Roll in dry flour and shallow fry. Serve with raw onions, tomato slices, cheese slices (optional) and lettuce sandwiched between burgher buns with a smear of mustard and ketchup. Alternately form into small balls and serve with raw onions and lemon slices with drinks as a snack. The balls after shallow frying may also be kept aside and made into a vegetarian 'kofta' curry.

ARMENIAN STUFFED CABBAGE

2 cups onions minced	¾ cup olive oil or, substitute
2-4 tblsp. parsley minced	1 large tomato chopped
1 cup small grained rice uncooked	1 medium tender cabbage
1 tsp. allspice/'*garam masala*' powder	½ -1 cup water or, as required
1-2 tsp. cinnamon powder	1 lemon juiced plus 1-2 tblsp. lemon juice (optional)
Salt, pepper and chilli/cayenne powder to taste	

Method

Fry the onions in the 2 tblsp. oil for about 15 minutes. Mix with the parsley, tomato and rice. Add the juice from one lemon and spices and mix well. This is the filling. Keep aside till required.

Place cabbage leaves one by one in salted boiling water and cook for 10 minutes till tender. Drain the water and pat the leaves dry with a tea towel. Cut the leaves in long strips, put in the filling and fold like 'samosas' in triangles. Line a buttered casserole with cabbage leaves and then arrange the triangles neatly over them. Pour ½ cup olive oil over the triangles and finally pour water to cover all. Press the triangles down with a plate placing a weight on the plate if necessary. Cover casserole and cook on medium heat till very soft. This should take around 1-1½ hours. Extra lemon juice may be added while cooking. When ready turn on to a flat dish. Sprinkle a little lemon juice and olive oil on top and serve. This is a good accompaniment with steaks or grilled/barbecued chicken, beef etc. or an excellent entrée for vegetarians.

Note. To cut down on cooking time microwave for 20-30 minutes or till ready on power 7. This dish can also be placed in a moderate oven for 45 minutes to 1 hour. However, it is best cooked on top of the stove or in a microwave oven.

SWISS CHARD SALAD

500 gm. Swiss chard stems only (The leaves may be put aside to be used as spinach later.

2 tsp. each mint and celery finely chopped

1 tsp. soya sauce

1 tsp. ketchup

4 tblsp. mayonnaise

2 tblsp. white wine

1½ tblsp. dry mustard powder or, paste
½ tsp. paprika (optional)

Salt & pepper to taste

Method

Wash and clean the stems of the Swiss chard by scraping with a knife. Cut each stem into four. Cook in boiling salted water for about 10 minutes. Drain and put in a bowl.

Make a sauce with the rest of the ingredients and pour over the Swiss chard stems and mix gently to coat. Chill. Serve in the bowl or on a bed of lettuce.

Variations: The above dressing could be used on slivers of left over roast or grilled chicken, cubes of steamed or grilled fish, sliced hard boiled eggs or any other vegetable or a combination of vegetables. Spinach with thick stems such as the Indian pooi (pooi saag) could be successful alternate substitutes. Those who have a penchant for brinjals may try it with the above dressing also. First roast the brinjal under the grill, top of the stove or in the oven. Peel skin and mash the pulp. Add dressing. Alternately the brinjal may be cut in slices lengthwise, gently rubbed with salt and shallow fried. Lay on a platter and pour dressing on top.

BREAD SALAD

1 medium head of lettuce	2-3 medium red tomatoes (not over ripe)
1 small onion minced (optional)	1-2 cloves garlic crushed or, ½ tsp. garlic powder
2-3 tblsp. French dressing	1 cup bread croutons

Method

Line a bowl with a few leaves of lettuce. Chop the rest of the lettuce roughly and put in the bowl. Cut tomatoes in wedges and add to the bowl. Sprinkle the onions and the garlic cloves if using. (If garlic powder is used, add it after the croutons). Add the bread croutons. Sprinkle 2-3 tblsp of French dressing on the salad and toss gently. It is advisable to assemble the salad just before serving or else it will become soggy. Garnish with a few sprigs of parsley.

SIMPLE TOMATO SALAD

4-5 medium tomatoes peeled and roughly chopped

1 tblsp. wine vinegar

1 tsp. dry mustard powder

½ tsp. paprika

Salt and pepper to taste

1-2 medium onions roughly chopped

1 tsp. sugar

1 green chilli chopped (optional)

½ tblsp. olive or salad oil

Method

Mix all together. Serve with any dish even curries.

Variation: Instead of wine use 1 tblsp. fresh lime juice. Substitute or add 1 tsp. garlic powder.

TABOULÉ

(This is a delicious popular Middle Eastern salad. There are slight changes in the various versions of the different regions but basically, they are all more or less all similar. This is an Israeli version.)

2 cups borghol (dalia) – very fine cracked wheat.	3 cups tomatoes chopped
Water for soaking borghol	1 medium lettuce
4 cups parsley chopped	4 cups onions minced
1 tblsp. salt or to taste	1 cup mint leaves chopped
¼ tsp. freshly ground pepper	1 tblsp. olive oil (preferably extra virgin)
¼ tsp. paprika or, chilli powder (optional)	1-2 fresh green chillis de-seeded and chopped (optional)
2 tblsp. fresh lemon juice	

Method

Put borghol in just enough water to cover and leave for approx. 1 hour. Drain all water and dry borghol with a tea towel. Spread on a tray and leave for approx. another 1 hour to dry off all moisture. Put borghol in a bowl with all the other ingredients except olive oil, lemon juice and lettuce and toss gently with a pair of salad spoon and fork. Line a salad bowl with a few leaves of lettuce. All the above can be prepared in advance. Just before serving add the oil and lemon juice to the borghol mixture and gently toss to mix. Put in the bowl lined with lettuce leaves and serve. The rest of the lettuce can be cut in bit size pieces and served in a separate bowl or plate. The salad bowl need not be lined with lettuce leaves. The borghol can go into the bowl by itself and the cut lettuce leaves can be had as an accompaniment. Serve with any meat or chicken dish or by itself with thick French or Italian bread. A bowl of garlic flavoured olive oil adds to the meal. The salad can be eaten with bits of the bread dipped in the garlic oil.

RUDJAK GENIT – INDONESIAN SALAD

4-5 slices pineapple cubed

1 large apple cubed

1-2 guavas de-seeded and cubed

1-2 pears cubed

1 medium cucumber de-seeded and cubed

1 medium carrot peeled and cubed

Sauce:

½ cup peanuts ground

2 tsp. sugar

1-2 tblsp. wine vinegar

1 tsp. paprika

1 tsp. salt or, to taste

Method

All the fruits and vegetables should be half ripe and crunchy. Any other fruits and vegetables can be substituted so long they blend well together. Combine the fruits and vegetables. Toss with the above sauce mixed together. Place in a salad bowl lined with lettuce and chill. A good accompaniment to any entree.

MELEZANA (GREEK AUBERGINE SALAD)

1 kg. aubergine

2 tblsp. vinegar/lemon juice

1 tsp. (or to taste) garlic minced

2-4 tblsp. olive oil

Salt and pepper to taste

Method

Roast aubergine on charcoal, under the grill or on a hot griddle till soft to get a smoky burnt taste. Cool and then discard the skin and as much of the seeds as possible. Mash the pulp and add all the other ingredients. Serve as an accompaniment with the main course or as a starter/hors d'oeuvres with cocktail wafer biscuits.

Variation:

1. Add the following to the mashed aubergine pulp – 1 egg yolk, 2 tblsp. lemon juice or to taste, salt & pepper to taste, 2-4 tblsp. olive oil and 1-2 tblsp parsley chopped fine.

2. The Israeli way is to add tahina (see under "Miscellaneous" in this book) according to taste. Garnish with chopped parsley.

GERMAN FARMER'S SALAD

1 lb. potatoes cooked, peeled and cubed

1-2 tblsp. vinegar/lemon juice (or half and half)

1 medium onion minced

2-4 tblsp. olive/salad oil

1 tsp. prepared mustard

½ tsp. paprika (optional)

6 oz. mushrooms chopped and sautéed or, 6 oz. corned beef/ham cubed (optional)

6-8 oz. tomatoes cubed

1 tsp. sugar

Salt and pepper to taste

1 tblsp. parsley chopped

Method

Toss the potatoes, corned beef/ham, tomatoes, and onion in a bowl. Mix the rest of the ingredients and add to the above gently. Serve on a bed of lettuce.

Variation: Left-over roast potatoes can be used in place of plain cooked potatoes or, part roast and part plain boiled potatoes may also be used.

Left over roast beef can be substituted instead of corned beef/ham.

APPLE SALAD

4 tblsp. olive oil

3-4 tblsp. red wine

Salt and pepper to taste

½ tsp. paprika

1 round head of lettuce cut in large bits

2 tblsp. lemon juice

1 small onion minced

1 tsp. sugar

1 large red apple grated unpeeled

1-2 tblsp. chives chopped

Method

Toss all the above ingredients together in a bowl. Garnish with the chives and serve immediately. Alternately keep all the sauce ingredients mixed and ready and add to the apple and lettuce just before serving or else the lettuce will get limp.

GREEN PAPAYA SALAD

2 cups green papaya grated

1 small capsicum grated fine

A pinch of paprika (optional)

2-4 tblsp. fresh lemon juice

Salt and pepper to taste

¼ tsp. fresh ginger minced (optional)

Method

Mix all the above ingredients together. The paprika gives it a good flavour. The ginger could be omitted. Serve this salad with any vegetarian or non-vegetarian curry, vegetarian burgers or kebabs, steaks, grilled chicken etc.

CHOLA/CHANA
(CHICKPEA OR GARBANZO BEAN) SALAD

½ cup chola soaked overnight

1 small cucumber diced

1 tblsp. lemon juice

½ tsp. green mint sauce

Salt and pepper to taste

¼ tsp. sugar

½ tsp. ginger shredded

¼ cup tender fresh corn kernels

1 small onion sliced in thin rings

¼ tsp. curry powder/'chaat masala/garlic powder

½ tsp. tomato and garlic sauce

¼ tsp. mustard

1 tblsp. red wine

½ tsp. light soya sauce

Method

Drain the chola and pat dry with a kitchen towel. Add the corn kernels, diced cucumber and onion rings, and stir all to mix. Next combine all the other ingredients in a bowl and then add to the chola mixture. Stir all together lightly to blend well. Line a flat dish or bowl with lettuce and pour the salad over it. Garnish with fresh green and red chillis and a few slices of onion rings.

Note: Instead of whole chola, the chola sprouts can also be used. Fresh corn kernels may be replaced with canned corn kernels. Use fresh chopped mint leaves instead of green mint sauce. In the absence of tomato garlic sauce make a paste of ketchup and fresh ground garlic or, garlic powder to taste.

INDIAN SALAD

250 gm. long stemmed tender spinach (pooi)	250 gm. mushrooms
1 tsp. whole fenugreek seeds	1 tsp. whole mustard seeds
1 large white radish julienned	2 medium thick carrots julienned
250 gm. French (green) beans julienned	250 gm. baby corn
1 tblsp. olive oil	1 tsp. lemon zest

Salt, pepper and paprika to taste

Method

Julienne the tender stems of the pooi keeping the leaves whole. Slice the mushrooms if large, otherwise keep them whole. Heat the oil slightly and add the fenugreek and mustard seeds. When they begin to splutter add the radish, carrots, beans and pooi stems. Stir for 1-2 minutes. Now add the pooi leaves, mushrooms, and baby corn. Stir for another 1-2 minutes. Add the seasonings and stir to mix. Take off heat and cool. Add the lemon zest and toss the salad gently. Refrigerate till required.

SPINACH & POTATO SALAD

½ cup mayonnaise

2 tblsp. cream

500 gm. potatoes boiled and cubed large

Salt and freshly ground pepper to taste

2 tblsp. 'kasundi' (strong Bengali mustard paste)

500 gm. any spinach steamed

½ tsp. sweet/hot paprika (optional)

Method

Combine the mayonnaise, 'kasundi', cream, paprika and seasoning to make the salad dressing. Toss the vegetables in the dressing and then refrigerate till required. If the spinach has large stems cut the tender stems in 2" lengths before steaming. Keep the spinach leaves whole.

CURRIED PASTA SALAD

1 tblsp. salad or olive oil	2 large onions thickly sliced
2 oz. cooked corn kernels	8 oz. cut macaroni cooked al denté
2 oz. cooked fresh green peas	2 tsp. curry powder
1 tsp. each coriander and cumin powder	1 large/medium green capsicum de-seeded and cut in thin strips
Salt and freshly ground black pepper to taste	1 large/medium red capsicum de-seeded and cut in thin strips
2 large red onion	

Method

Heat the oil a little and sauté the onion till the colour changes. Add all the above cooked ingredients. Stir once and then add all the spices. Mix well and cook for 4-5 minutes on moderate heat till there is a nice aroma and the pasta is well coated with the spices. Add the peppers and seasoning. Toss well with the pasta on low heat for a further 4-5 minutes. Sprinkle a little water only if necessary to prevent pasta from sticking to the pan. Take off heat, cool and keep in the refrigerator till required. Can also be served hot.

Variations:

1. 4 oz. cottage cheese or *tofu* cut in cubes and slightly browned can be added during the last minute of cooking, before adding the capsicums.
2. Add ½-1 tsp turmeric powder with the spices to give a more yellow and "curryish" colour.

FISH & SEAFOOD

GRILLED FISH

[This recipe is best with medium sized whole fish with the head and tail on or, large fillets. The fish should not be too bony — just a centre bone.]

Fish — 1 to 1½ kg.

Make gashes on both sides, width wise without cutting through

Marinade:

1 large onion	3-4 cloves of garlic
1" piece ginger	1 tsp. cumin powder
1 tsp. coriander	2 tbsp. tomato sauce
2-3 tbsp. oil	1 tbsp. dark vinegar

Salt and pepper to taste

1 tbsp. Worcester sauce or, any black sauce or, dark soy sauce or, fish/anchovy sauce.

(Good combinations are: (I) tomato, fish and Worcester sauce, (ii) soy sauce only, (iii) any black sauce, tomato sauce. (iv)] only barbeque sauce.

Method

Marinate fish in the above 2-3 hours rubbing it well into the fish. Grill under gas or electric grill though charcoal grilling has the best effect. When grilling under gas or electric flame, place fish in the lowest rung under low heat. This will take a little longer to cook but will have a better effect. Brush fish with left-over marinade from time to time. Turn over carefully when one side done and proceed in a similar way. Each side should take 5-10 minutes to cook, depending on the freshness of the fish. Frozen fish needs more careful handling when grilling as it could break easily. When fish is ready, lay on a long flat serving dish.

Sauce:

Scrape marinade from grilling pan using a little hot water if necessary. If sauce is to be served separately or, poured over the fish, add a little more water, about 1 cup. If sauce is too weak, add a little more of the bottled sauce and taste for the right flavour. Thicken with 1 tbsp. of corn starch.

To serve:

Surround fish with the following: Rice. In a large saucepan warm 1 tbsp. oil, fry 1-2 large, sliced onions till golden brown. Add a bunch of chopped spring onions. Mix well. Next add 1 cup boiled rice. Stir. Add fish marinade (optional) and mix well. Lay chopped ham/smoked ham or bacon, and sliced boiled eggs or, omelette on top of the rice.

MOCK GRILLED FISH

1 kg. fish fillet

1 tblsp. sweet red wine

1 tblsp. A-1, barbecue, or any other black sauce

2-3 potatoes sliced

2 tblsp. or more oil

1-2 tblsp. ketchup

Salt and pepper to taste

1 medium green pepper de-seeded and sliced (optional)

2 tsp. anchovy or, any fish sauce

Method

Clean and pat dry fish fillet. Keep it whole or cut in serving pieces. Mix all the above ingredients in a bowl and pour over fish. Let fish marinate in this mixture for an hour. Next lay fish in a wide fry pan along with the marinade, potatoes and green pepper and cook on low heat. Turn fish, potatoes, and green pepper once, spooning the marinade over from time to time as and when required. Continue cooking till potatoes are done. Serve hot with a green, rice or a pasta salad.

FISH PIE

Filling:

500 gm. Fish – steamed and mashed

1 cup (or more) white sauce

1 tblsp. anchovy or fish sauce

Salt and pepper to taste

1 bunch spring onion – minced fine

1 bunch parsley – chopped

1 egg separated

Method

Mix all the ingredients. Bind with egg yolk. Beat egg white stiff. Fold into fish mixture. Make short-crust pastry to line a 9" flat dish. Do not make pastry too thick. Bake in hot oven for 15 minutes. Take out. Sprinkle with breadcrumbs. Put fish filling. Return to oven and bake till set.

Serve with a salad.

BAR-B-Q WHOLE FISH WITH COCONUT SAUCE

This is best made with fish that has just one middle bone and not too many bones on the side. But the fish must be tasty! This is best served with "*Tandoori Roti*" homemade (see bread chapter of the book) or from one of many favourite shops.

2-3 kg. whole fish well cleaned

½ cup lime juice or more

Salt, pepper, and chilli powder to taste

¼ cup or less melted ghee

Method

Make a few diagonal gashes on both sides of the fish so the marinade can penetrate inside. Marinate fish in a mixture of lime juice, salt, pepper, and chilli powder for several hours or leave overnight in the refrigerator. Barbecue or grill sprinkling ghee from time to time to get a smoky flavour. When ready lay on a flat dish and pour sauce over it. Garnish with fresh chopped or a few sprigs of coriander leaves.

Sauce:

3-4 medium tomatoes

1 large bulb garlic

½ - 1 tsp. turmeric powder

1½ - 2 cups very thick coconut milk

Liquidize tomatoes, garlic, more salt & pepper if necessary and turmeric for colour. Cook all together in a saucepan till dry. Now pour the coconut milk over it, stir, then simmer on low heat till thick.

Variations:

The sauce could be served separately with the fish instead of pouring over it. In this case, lay fish on a platter, pour some more melted ghee over it while still hot and garnish with sliced onions, sliced lime, grated carrot and sprigs of fresh coriander leaves.

Again, this makes a great party fare which is easy to assemble. The fish could be grilled or barbecued a little before dinner time, then warmed in the oven just before serving with sauce and garnish over it or separately.

SIMPLE BAKED FISH

8 oz. white fish

1-2 egg separated

2-4 tblsp. cheese (preferably parmesan) grated

1 cup white sauce

1 tblsp. fresh parsley minced fine

1 oz. butter

Method

Poach fish and then flake with a fork. Make the white sauce as given below. Take off heat and add 1-2 egg yolks. Blend the yolks one by one into the sauce with a wooden spoon thoroughly after each addition. Next mix the parsley and cheese, reserving a little to sprinkle on top, into the sauce. Now add the fish to the sauce stirring gently to mix. Last of all beat the egg whites stiff and fold into the fish mixture. Transfer fish to an oven proof dish. Sprinkle top with grated cheese and dot with butter. Bake in a moderately hot oven till top is a golden brown. Serve with creamy mash potato and a salad or steamed mixture of vegetables (peas, green beans, and carrots) tossed in a little butter and fresh finely chopped mint leaves.

White Sauce:

1 oz. butter

1 tblsp. flour heaped

A pinch of mustard powder

1 small onion minced

1 cup milk

Salt and pepper to taste

Blend butter, onion, and flour in a saucepan over low heat. Add milk and keep stirring with a wooden spoon till mixture begins to thicken. Take off heat and add the seasonings stirring to mix. The mixture should be smooth with no lumps. Keep aside till required.

BAKED TOMATO FISH

500 gm fish fillet (bekti, mackerel, king fish, blue fish etc. are suitable	½ cup or more flour
2 whole garlic or more minced	2-3 onions minced
250 gm. tomatoes chopped	2 tsp. cayenne pepper
Salt and pepper to taste	3-4 extra tomatoes chopped small
4 tblsp. oil	1-2 capsicum or, spring onions (optional)

Method

Cut the fillets into serving pieces. Next cut each piece of fish into four. Clean and pat dry fish pieces with paper towels. Roll the pieces in the dry flour to coat well. Fry the fish in oil a golden brown. Drain on paper towels and keep aside. In a pan heat 2 tsp oil and sauté the garlic and onion. When the colour changes add the tomatoes, cayenne, salt & pepper and cook for a few minutes till mushy and like a sauce. Take off heat. Grease an oven proof dish and lay the fish pieces in a single row. Pour the sauce over it spreading it out evenly. Cover with extra chopped tomatoes, capsicum, or spring onions or both. Bake in a moderately hot oven till done. Serve with steamed rice, a potato or pasta salad.

GUYANESE BAKED FISH IN WINE

2 spring onions or, 1 small onion chopped

¾ cup mushroom sliced

1 kg. fish fillet

1 cup dry white wine

2 tblsp. white sauce

¼ cup cream

Salt and pepper to taste

1 tblsp. spring onions chopped for garnish

1 tblsp. fresh parsley chopped for garnish

Method

Butter an oven proof dish liberally. Arrange spring onions/onions and mushrooms at the base. Sprinkle with salt & pepper. Place filet on top. Pour wine over fish. Cover with buttered foil. Bake in a moderate oven till fish flakes easily when tested with a fork. Drain juices from the dish to a saucepan. Cook over medium heat till the liquid is reduced to half the quantity. Now add the white sauce and cream and cook on low heat rotating the pan continuously till the sauce thickens. Pour the sauce over the fish which has been transferred to a flat dish. Garnish with the chopped spring onions and parsley.

Serve with steamed and buttered rice, peas, and carrots all together. The fish can also be surrounded with the rice mixture like a border.

GUYANESE BAKED FISH SUPREME

6 fish fillets skinned and de-boned

6 slices of cheese (cheddar or substitute)

1 oz. or, I tblsp. flour

2 small onions chopped

2 tblsp. dry sherry

Salt and pepper to taste

6 slices tomatoes

1 oz. butter or margarine

½ pint or, 10 oz. milk

6-8 oz. button mushrooms

1-2 tblsp. or more chopped parsley for garnish

Method

Rub fish fillets with salt and pepper. Dust off excess. Arrange fillets, tomato, and cheese slices alternately in a shallow oven proof dish. Melt margarine in a saucepan over low heat. Stir in flour sifted with salt to taste. Add the milk a little at a time along with all the rest of the ingredients. Keep stirring mixture until it starts to boil. Take off heat and pour over the fillets. Bake in a moderate oven for about 20 minutes or until the fish is cooked. Garnish the top with parsley. Serve hot with plain steamed or buttered rice.

FISH CHOPS - ECONOMICAL

500 gm. fish fillet, preferably bekti, mackerel, or fish with less bones	1 tblsp. oil
1 large onion chopped	1 tsp. garlic juice
1 tsp. fresh ginger juice	1 tblsp. yogurt/tomato-purée or ketchup
½ tsp. turmeric (optional)	1 tsp. fresh *garam masala* powder
A few raisins	Milk or water
4 slices of bread	1 tsp. freshly roasted ground cumin
500 gm. boiled or mashed potatoes	Salt and pepper to taste

Method

Filling:

Steam and flake fish fillets with a fork. Cook in oil with onion, ginger, garlic, and turmeric, if using. Add yoghurt or tomato puree/ketchup and mix well. Add raisins when ready, cover and let cook with fish for a few seconds till they swell up very slightly. Just before taking off the heat, remove cover and sprinkle with garam masala powder and mix well.

Potato Casing:

Soak bread in a shallow dish with water or milk just to cover for 1 minute and then squeeze out liquid by pressing bread with both hands. Blend bread with mashed potatoes. Add ground cumin and salt to taste. Make 12-15 oblong shapes with mixture. Put in filling and cover well. Roll in bread crumb and either deep or shallow fry. Serve with green salad.

BENGALI FISH CHOP

Potato casing:

250 gm. Potatoes	1 tsp. ground turmeric
3 tsp. ground ginger	2 tsp. ground cumin
2 tsp. ground coriander	1 tblsp. yogurt
1 tsp. garam masala powder	

Fish filling:

1 kg. fish	Chilli powder to taste
1 tblsp. ground onion	1 tblsp. tomato purée
4-5 tblsp. oil	Salt to taste

Method

Steam fish in pressure-cooker 5 minutes. When cool flake wit a fork. In oil fry fish with all the ingredients under 'fish filling' except *garam masala*. Make sure fish is well cooked and blended with all the ingredients. Should be mushy. Before taking off heat, sprinkle garam masala powder.

Boil and mash potatoes. Fry in oil with the ingredients under potatoes. Mix fish and potato mixture well. Make into round or oblong shapes. Do not make them too thick or too thin. Roll in beaten egg and breadcrumbs and either deep or shallow fry in the remainder oil. Add more oil, if necessary for deep frying.

Variations

1. Spread a large plate with sifted flour. Roll chops in the flour to coat all sides. Let stand for 1½ hours. Shallow fry slowly in a large fry-pan on low heat

2. Whether deep or shallow frying in egg or breadcrumbs or, plain flour, the chops can be filled with any of the following mixtures, if so desired:

i. A mixture of chopped coriander leaves and onions or, plain coriander leaves.

ii. Chopped mint or basil or parsley leaves or chopped spring onions.

iii. Finely chopped celery stem or leaves. Do not over fill with celery as the flavour could be overbearing.

iv. <u>Shrimp filling</u>. Mixed and sautéed with finely minced spring onions. Or, sautéed with finely sliced onions with a dash of cumin or coriander powder OR cook shrimps with a little onion and ginger juice, adding a few chopped coriander leaves. OR those with a penchant for a garlic flavour, cook shrimps in a little oil, add ketchup and chilli powder, garlic powder and salt to taste. Add chopped green capsicum (optional).

v. <u>Mushroom filling</u>. Cook any kind of mushrooms chopped with onions or spring onions with a dash of Worcestershire sauce.

CURRIED FISH CAKES

500 gm. steamed and mashed fish	1 cup basic white sauce
1 heaped tsp. curry powder	Salt and pepper to taste
2 tblsp. chopped coriander leaves fresh or dried (If using dried leaves, soak in warm water for a few minutes, drain, wipe, dry and use).	Chilli powder to taste (optional)

Method

Make <u>White Sauce</u>. Remove from heat. Add curry powder, chilli powder and coriander leaves. Mix well.

Add fish to sauce and blend well. If sauce is too thin, cook a while longer till dry enough to form fish cakes. Take off heat. Cool. Shape into rounds with a standard size jam jar lid. Fill lid with mixture, pat top evenly with a spatula or flat knife. Invert on a plate of flour. Coat both sides. Dip in beaten egg (1-2 eggs) or, a mixture of egg and water (1 egg and 2 tbsp. water), roll in breadcrumbs. Deep fry in oil. Serve with crisp *potato juliennes*, sprinkled over, and assorted steamed and buttered mixed vegetables — peas, carrots, green beans, and corn kernels.

Potato julienne:

Peel potato, grate into threads, or put in the food processor. Deep fry.

FISH ROLL

500 gm. fish fillets cut into serving pcs.	Salt and pepper to taste
1-2 tblsp. lime juice	½ cup flour
1-2 eggs slightly beaten	1 cup breadcrumbs
½ cup oil for frying	

Method

Beat the fish pieces with the back of a knife or meat tenderizer gently to make it almost double in size without damaging or cutting it through. Rub the pieces with salt and pepper and soak in lime juice for 5-10 minutes. Pat dry with paper towel. Put any of the following fillings and roll flattened fish pieces like sausages the size of an index finger. Dust with dry flour and rest for a few minutes. Next dip in egg and then roll in breadcrumbs repeating the process twice. Again, rest for a few minutes. Heat oil and gently fry the rolls turning constantly so that they are an even golden brown. Drain on paper towels. The rolls may also be shallow fried in a heavy bottomed fry pan on low heat which, though takes a little longer is better for the health conscious. Serve with a green or tomato/cucumber salad with a vinegar, mustard, sugar, salt, and pepper dressing.

Filling:

1 tsp. oil	1 onion minced
2 tsp. onion paste	1 tsp each of ginger and garlic paste
1-2 tblsp. of ground coconut	A handful of raisins
1 tsp. each of coriander and cumin powder	1-2 tblsp. fresh coriander leaves
1 Green chilli minced (optional)	

1. In oil fry the minced onions and then the spices and coconut till no raw smell lingers. Take off heat, add the coriander leaves and chillis if using and mix.

2. To the above mixture add 1-2 tblsp shrimps and fry with the spices. The coconut may be omitted.
3. A combination of cooked chopped plain or smoked ham and grated cheese also makes a good filling. In this case no need to cook the filling or add any other ingredients.

Variation:

Instead of frying the rolls in breadcrumbs dip them in the following batter, deep fry, drain on paper towels and serve with a salad.

Batter:

  2 cups flour   1 tsp. heaped baking powder

  Salt and pepper to taste   1-2 eggs

  Milk for mixing

Mix and sift the dry ingredients. Add the egg/eggs one at a time and stir with a wooden spoon. Add enough milk for a thick batter of pouring consistency. Let rest for half hour.

MASALA OR SPICY POMFRET

(The recipe can be used for "serving size" whole pomfret one per head or, 1 or 2 large pomfrets which later can be cut for serving.)

4 tblsp. oil	¼ cup onion paste
1 tsp. ginger paste	½ tsp. garlic paste
1 tsp. red chilli powder (optional)	1 tsp. turmeric
500 gm. pomfret – make gashes with a knife width wise without cutting all the way through – as for grilling	2 large banana leaves

Method

Fry spices in heated oil (reserving 2 tsp.) well. Remove from heat. Apply paste well on fish, filling in the gashes and inside the belly. Put 2 tsp. oil in a wide heavy bottom pan. Line with banana leaves. Place fish on them — do not let them overlap. Cover with more banana leaves. Place lid on pan on top and cook on low heat for 15-20 minutes or till fish done.

Variation

In the absence of banana leaves use aluminium foil. However, banana leaves give the dish that extra flavour.

MALAYSIAN STUFFED FISH

2 kg. bekti (or any other fish with just one centre bone)

1 tsp. turmeric powder

Oil for frying

Chilli powder to taste

Salt to taste

Method

Clean and wash fish well. Pat dry with paper towels. If fish is too large for frying, then fillet the fish and cut in large pieces. Rub fish with the above ingredients and stuff with the filling given below. Secure well with toothpicks or, a paste of flour and water. Fry fish with just enough oil for it to rest on. Turn over gently when one side is done. Drain well on paper towels. Served with any salad or a mixture of seasonal vegetables cooked in coconut milk.

Filling:

1 tblsp. grated coconut

2 tblsp. coriander leaves chopped

1-2 tblsp. water

1-2 tblsp. lemon juice

Salt to taste

1 tsp. sugar

Liquidize the first four ingredients. Strain the excess water. Add the next two ingredients and mix well. The filling is now ready for stuffing the fish.

TANGY FISH

500 gm. Filleted bekti (or similar fish)

2 tblsp. ketchup

2 tblsp. wine vinegar

1 tblsp. Worcester sauce

2 tblsp. dark soya sauce

2 tblsp; red wine (optional), not needed if wine vinegar is used

2 tblsp. salad or olive oil

½ tsp. pepper

1 tsp. fresh or dried tarragon leaves

Salt to taste

2 tblsp. water

Method

Place all above ingredients except fish and water in a bowl. (Cut fish fillet in 6-8 or more serving pieces). Place fish in a non-stick wide fry-pan. Pour mixture in bowl over fish evenly. Wash bowl with water and pour over fish. Place fry-pan on low heat and cook till fish is done. The fish should have a thick gravy just enough to cover it. Serve with mashed potatoes or surround with boiled rice. Also serve a tomato or cucumber salad or, boiled peas or, whole boiled cabbage.

Variations

1. Add 1-2 tsp. curry powder to the mixture in the bowl.
2. A chicken or beef bouillon cube (crumbled) may also be added to the mixture with or without the curry powder.
3. If serving boiled vegetable — smear 1 tbsp. melted butter or margarine, if so desired. Next sprinkle fresh chopped herbs e.g. parsley, mint, basil. For cabbage, can sprinkle caraway or dill seeds.

LEMON GARLIC BUTTER FISH

1 lb. fish fillet cut in serving pieces

1 tblsp. (or less) garlic paste

Salt and pepper to taste

4-6 tblsp. olive oil

¼ cup (more or less) fresh lemon juice

2-4 tblsp. butter

Method

Marinate fish pieces in the garlic paste, seasoning and olive oil for 1 hr. Slightly heat a non-stick, heavy bottom or grill pan. Lay the fish pieces with the marinade in the pan without them over lapping. When one side done turn the fish over and cook the other side. Now pour lemon juice mixed with melted butter over the fish. Let fish soak in the sauce for a few seconds. Remove from heat and serve garnished with parsley. Serve with small whole sautéed potatoes and steamed mixed vegetables e.g. carrots, peas, green beans, and cauliflower.

FISH IN GARLIC & TOMATO SAUCE

250 gm. fish fillet cut in thin frying slices	1 tsp. lemon juice
2-3 tblsp. corn flour	1 egg white slightly beaten
3-4 tblsp. oil	Salt and pepper to taste

Method

Sprinkle fish slices with lemon juice, salt, and pepper. Leave to stand for about 1 hr. Add enough corn flour to beaten egg white to make a fairly thick batter. Dip fish in this batter till well coated. Fry gently till crisp. Remove from heat. Drain off excess oil from pan. Replace fish in the pan and pour the following sauce over it. Cook over gentle heat for about 2-3 minutes. Serve on a bed of light fried rice. Sprinkle with a mild grated cheese.

Sauce:

1 cup chicken stock or, 1 chicken/vegetarian bouillon cube diluted in 1 cup warm water	½ tsp. or more garlic powder
1 small bay leaf	1 1-2 tblsp. tomato purée
Salt and pepper to taste	

Mix all the above in a saucepan and cook on low heat for about 5 minutes. Pour over fish and cook for another couple of minutes as mentioned above.

Fried Rice:

2 tblsp. oil	2 onions sliced
1 cup left over or freshly cooked rice	1/3 cup cooked green peas
3-4 French green beans or, 2 long Indian beans (borboti) cut in 1" lengths	1 medium carrot
1 capsicum cut in thin strips	4-5 strands spring onion cut in thin strips

1 tsp. soy sauce	2 tsp. sherry or red wine

Salt and pepper to taste

Heat oil. Stir fry all vegetables except capsicum and spring onions. After 5 minutes add the capsicum and spring onions. Cook another 2 minutes. Add the rice. Stir soy sauce, wine, and seasoning. Stir all well. and take off heat. The vegetables should not be overdone. they should be half cooked and crunchy. Garnish with thin strips of omelette, parsley/coriander leaves.

FISH & MUSHROOM IN WINE SAUCE

500 gm. fish fillet (bekti, mackerel, fish, with less bones and thick white meat)	2 egg whites
1 heaped tblsp. corn flour	2 tblsp. oil
2 large onions	1 large bunch of spring onions
1 green capsicum (optional)	200 gm. Fresh mushroom
Salt and pepper to taste	

Sauce:

1 cup warm water	1 chicken bouillon cube
2 tblsp. sweet red wine	2 tblsp. corn flour
Salt and pepper to taste	

Method

Cut fish fillets into small cubes. Coat in a mixture of egg white, corn flour, salt, and pepper. Fry lightly in shallow pan or non-stick pan. Keep fish aside. In same pan, add a little more oil if necessary (not too much). Stir fry lightly, largely sliced onions, chopped spring onions, capsicum seeded, thinly sliced, and then quartered, and thickly sliced mushrooms (if using button mushrooms, keep whole). When onions become translucent (must not brown), add the sauce, which has been pre-mixed, all together in a bowl. Cook over low heat a few minutes, stirring constantly. When vegetables are soft, add fish and cook a few minutes longer to let sauce penetrate fish.

Serve with soft, creamy mashed potatoes made into a wall on a flat long dish. Place fish in the centre. Garnish with finely chopped spring onions, sprinkled on top. As accompaniments, serve a good salad of your choice and mashed garlic aubergine. (See under 'vegetable section' of the book.)

Variations

For added flavour, mix 1-2 yolks of eggs to the sauce. Be sure, the yolks are well blended with the sauce and do not curdle during cooking.

FISH IN ORIENTAL WHITE SAUCE

500 gm. bekti or any white fish fillet cut into 8-10 serving pieces

4 tblsp. oil

1 tsp. black cumin whole

1 tblsp. flour – sieved

1 cup water

Salt to taste

2-3 green chillis (optional)

Method

Fry fish to a golden colour in 3 tblsp. oil. Drain and keep aside. In the saucepan add remainder 1 tbsp. oil. When warm put in cumin seeds. When they start sputtering, pour in flour and water, mixed well. When it comes to boil, lay fish in it. Add salt and green chilies (if using) slit at the sides with seeds taken out. Cook covered 5 minutes till fish absorbs gravy. Sprinkle chopped coriander leaves, stir once, and take off heat. Serve with buttered boiled rice and peas.

Variations

1. Instead of a white sauce, you can make a yellow sauce. After the black cumin seeds start spluttering, add 2 tsp. turmeric powder, salt to taste mixed in 1 cup water and a few whole green chilies according to taste. When it starts to boil, add the fish, and cook a few more minutes to let the gravy penetrate the fish. Make a smooth paste of 1 tbsp. flour with a little cold water. Add to fish to thicken gravy. Keep stirring ensuring no lumps are formed.

2. Instead of keeping fried fish aside, pour flour water mixture on fish. Add salt and green chilies as above. Cover and cook for 5 minutes. Remove from heat. In a small pan put in 1 tbsp. oil. Warm and add b lack cumin seeds. When spluttering starts, pour over fish, and return to heat. Cook 2 minutes uncovered and then add coriander leaves as above.

3. Warm 1 tsp. oil. add 1 bay leaf. When it browns, add pre-cooked rice and peas. Toss well and serve with fish.

ANCHOVY ROLL

Casing:

3 heaped tblsp. margarine/butter   ¾ cup flour

¼ tsp. baking powder   2 cups milk

4 eggs

Filling:

11¼ oz. anchovies   8 oz. chopped onions

1 tblsp. margarine/butter

Method

Casing:

Melt margarine in a heavy-bottomed saucepan. Add flour and baking powder sifted together as for white sauce and cook on low heat for 2-3 minutes. Add milk, stir, and cook till thick and smooth. Remove from heat and cool slightly. Separate egg yolks and whites. Add 1 egg yolk at a time beating after each addition. Beat egg whites stiff and fold into mixture. Butter a large sheet of grease-proof paper and place on a baking tray. Pour mixture on it. Smoothen out with a spatula to a 13" × 9" oblong strip. Bake for 20 minutes at 220^0 C. Do not open the oven door for the first 10 minutes.

Filling:

Clean and skin anchovies. Cut with kitchen scissors into small pieces. Sauté onions in margarine till soft. Add anchovy pieces and a little of the juice. Cook till mushy.

When batter is ready, take out of oven and put in the filling. Roll like a Swiss roll while still hot. Serve whole or cut in slices. Do not let batter be too hard or it will be difficult to roll. Serve with any kind of salad. This could be a first course or, a main course for supper, in which case, serve with creamy mashed potatoes in addition to the salad. This can also be served as one of the dishes on the buffet table. Cut in thin slices it could also be served with drinks as a snack.

Variations

1. In the absence of anchovies, use any other small fish e.g. smelt etc. Steam in the steamer or pressure cook till bones are dissolved and easy to pull out. or, after steaming, put through the food processor to break and dissolve the bones. Add 1 tbsp. anchovy or fish sauce and 1 tbsp. ketchup (optional) and then proceed to cook as the filling above.

2. Shrimps may also be used. Clean, shell and remove tail, head, and black thread at the spine. Throw away the tails but reserve the heads. Steam the shrimps and cut up small. Proceed as per filling. Pressure cook the heads till very tender. Process or liquidize. Next strain through a fine mesh or muslin. Use this instead of anchovy juice when using a shrimp filling. Any left-over prawn juice could be stored in the freezer to be used in flavouring any other prawn or fish dish at a future date.

3. Smoked cooked ham, smoked cooked sausage or, Chinese sausage cooked with onions and bechamel sauce would also make a good filling. Make sure the ham or sausage is finely chopped. If using Chinese sausages — pressure cook and then mince or put through a food processor. Sprinkle bunch of chopped parsley just before taking off the heat in the case of ham or sausages.

POTATO CHOPS WITH ROE FILLING

8 oz. (or more) roe steamed and crumbled	1 large onion minced or, 2 tblsp. Spring onions minced
2 tsp. anchovy sauce or, fish sauce	1 tblsp. ketchup or, tomato paste
1 capsicum or, I green chilli minced	Salt to 6taste
6-8 medium potatoes cooked and mashed	¼ cup flour or as required
1 cup breadcrumbs or, as required	2-3 eggs blended with 2-3 tblsp. milk or water
Oil for frying	

Method

Mix the roe with the onions, sauces, chillis and seasoning to make a filling. Make several flat cakes (the size of a jam jar lid or a little smaller), with the mashed potato. Place some filling in the centre. Draw and cover up with the potato from the sides to either form oval or round chops. The potato casing should be kept thin. Roll in dry flour and let them rest for 10-15 minutes. Dip in egg mixture and roll in breadcrumbs. Repeat this once more and again let the chops rest for 10-15 minutes after shaking off excess crumbs. Shallow or deep fry in oil. Serve with any sauce, dip, chutney, or pickle.

Variations:

<u>*Roe Cakes*</u> - Make the filling as above omitting the capsicum and adding 1-2 tblsp fresh chopped coriander leaves. The green chillis may be added if desired. Make into small flat cakes like fish cakes and fry as the potato chops above.

Instead of dipping chops or cakes in egg before frying, a paste of flour and water of the same consistency as egg can be substituted.

ROE PUDDING

2 tblsp. butter	2 tblsp. flour
1 large onion minced	1½ cup milk
Salt and pepper to taste	½ tsp. paprika (optional)
2 eggs separated	4 tblsp. cheddar grated
8 oz. roe steamed	1-2 tblsp. breadcrumbs

Method

Make white sauce by heating butter, flour and onions over low flame stirring continuously till butter melts. Add the milk gradually and continue to stir till sauce begins to thicken. Take off heat and add the seasonings. Now add the yolks one at a time and beat to mix well. Fold in 3 tblsp cheese. Now mix in the steamed roe. Last of all fold in gently the whites of eggs beaten stiffly. Pour into a greased oven proof dish. Spread top with the remaining cheese and breadcrumbs. Bake in a moderate oven till slightly set and the top turns golden. The pudding should not be too dry. Serve with baked mashed potatoes and a green salad.

LEMON FISH

500 gm. fish fillet	2 tblsp. butter/margarine/oil
1 small onion minced	2 tblsp. flour
1 cup milk or, ½ milk and ½ water	Salt and pepper to taste
1 sweet red pepper de-seeded and minced	1 tsp. fresh/dried thyme leaves
1 tsp. fresh/dried tarragon leaves	1-2 tblsp. lemon juice
1 tblsp. mayonnaise	Parsley for garnish
1-2 tsp. lemon zest	

Method

Steam fish fillet whole or cut in large pieces. Lay on a flat serving dish. Make a lemon sauce as under and pour over fish. Garnish with fresh parsley leaves. Serve with boiled and sliced potatoes tossed in butter and sprinkled with chopped mint/parsley OR surround fish with a border/wall of creamy mashed potatoes. Also serve a bowl of mixed vegetables as in "Easy Baked Fish"

Lemon Sauce:

Make a white sauce as in "Easy Baked Fish" with the above ingredients. Add the red pepper and herbs. Take off heat and cool slightly. Add the mayonnaise and blend into the sauce. Next add the lemon juice and zest and stir to mix.

SMOTHERED LOBSTER OR CRAYFISH MEAT

2-4 tblsp. butter

1 tsp. tomato purée

1 cup tomatoes peeled and chopped fine

2 tblsp. fresh parsley chopped

Salt and pepper to taste

2 tblsp. celery chopped fine

2 tblsp. spring onion chopped fine (optional)

1½ tblsp. flour

1 cup fish stock

1-1½ cup meat of lobster, crayfish or prawn chopped roughly

1-2 (or more) cloves garlic minced fine

A large pinch of cayenne pepper or paprika

1 cup onion chopped fine

Method

Melt butter in a heat proof casserole or saucepan. Remove from heat and stir in the flour till well blended and smooth. Return to heat and continue stirring till roux is a deep brown – approx. 5-8 minutes. Add the tomato puree to the fish stock and then stir into the roux. Next add the tomatoes, lobster meat or substitute, parsley, garlic, seasonings, onions, celery, and spring onion. Let all come to the boil once, reduce heat, cover, and simmer for 15–20 minutes or till done. It should be of a creamy consistency. Serve surrounded by hot buttered rice and a green salad.

Note

If desired the meat from the shellfish can be either pre-cooked in boiling water, pressure cooked, in the oven or under the grill. If cooked under the grill or oven smear shellfish with a little oil

----

SEAFOOD CREOLE STYLE

2-4 tblsp. butter or olive oil

1 cup celery chopped

4-6 cloves of garlic chopped

2-3 bay leaves

½-¾ cup green pepper chopped

1 tsp. gourmet powder (optional)

1-1½ cup or more water

1½ cup cooked crab meat chunks

2 tblsp. flour

1-1½ cups onion chopped

1 cup okra diced (optional)

3 cups headless shrimps cleaned

1-2 tsp. cayenne/paprika/tabasco

2-3 cups tomatoes chopped

2-3 tblsp. fresh parsley chopped

Salt and pepper to taste

1 cup white fish fillets cubed

Method

Heat butter/oil in a heavy-bottomed pan. Sauté onion till soft. Add celery and okra (if using) till light brown. Add the garlic and cook for another 1 min. Now add the shrimp and cook for about 2-3 minutes till opaque. Add all the other ingredients except the fish, crab, and flour. Bring the whole to a boil. Lower heat and simmer for about 5-10 mins   Now add the fish and cook till fish is done. Add the crab, stir gently, and cook for about 1-2 minutes. Thicken with the flour made into a paste with some cold water and keep stirring so no lumps form. Take off heat and serve on a bed of plain boiled rice.

Variation:

Add 1 or ½ a cup of chopped cooked ham with the crab. If preferred the shrimps can be added at the same time as the fish.

HUNGARIAN FISH (RĀC)

1 whole fish with only a central bone (approx. 1½ - 2 kg.)

2 large onions

8 oz. oil

¼ pt. or more medium dry red wine

Salt and black pepper to taste

Preparation

The fish should not have too many bones, just one central bone. Keep the head and skin intact. Clean, wash and pat fish dry. Chop and liquidize onion.

Method

Rub fish with salt, pepper, and onions well. Place on a baking tray. Pour the oil and then the wine over it. Cook in a medium hot oven. Baste with oil and wine liquid in the tray from time to time. Just before serving, brown both sides under the grill.

Serve garnished with lemon wedges, accompanied by creamy mashed potatoes *au gratin* and a green or tomato salad.

Variation

Instead of potatoes serve with plain buttered rice and sautéed mixed vegetables.

CHINESE FISH

8 pcs. fish for frying	1 egg
1 tblsp. coriander	2½ tblsp. oil
1 large onion	1 medium capsicum
1-2 oz. bamboo shoots	4 oz. French green beans
4 tblsp. chopped spring onions	1 large size bacon
2 tsp. dark soya sauce	1 bouillon cube
2-3 cups of water	½ tsp. black pepper
Pinch of ajinomoto/gourmet powder/ sugar	Salt to taste

Method

Fish to be sliced thin suitable for frying. Dip fish in beaten egg and dredge with corn flour. Fry crisp in 2 tbsp. oil, drain and keep aside. In a *wok* or deep-frying pan, warm the remainder 2 tbsp. oil. Fry the onion cut in large slices. When it changes colour add de-seeded coarsely chopped capsicum, thinly sliced bamboo shoots, thinly sliced beans cut at a slant, chopped (about ¼") spring onions and coarsely chopped bacon. Stir fry all the above vegetables for a few minutes. In a separate small bowl, mix soy sauce, bouillon cube, water, salt, and black pepper. Pour over vegetables and cook about 2-3 minutes. Lay fish gently over vegetable and cook a further few more minutes till liquid penetrates the fish. Before taking off heat, add ajinomoto or substitute. Serve surrounded by cooked Chinese egg noodles or rice.

Variations

1. Can sprinkle an extra crumbled, crisply fried bacon or just plain ham.
2. Fried crumbled Chinese sausages sprinkled over also gives an added flavour.

FISH IN BLACK BEAN SAUCE

500-750 gm. Fish fillet	2-4 tblsp. corn flour or, 2 tblsp. plain white flour
2 oz. black soy or moong beans	4 tblsp. Oil
1 tsp. fresh ginger minced	2 tsp. brandy
1 tsp. light soy sauce	4-5 spring onions chopped in ¼" bits
1 slice bacon (optional)	½ pt. water
Salt to taste	

Method

Mix salt with 3½ tblsp. of corn flour or, 2 tblsp. flour. Coat fish well with the dry ingredients. Steam the black beans. They should be soft but not mushy. Do not let the skin come off.

Fry fish pieces in oil a golden colour. Drain, keep aside. Pour off excess oil if any, leaving just 1 tsp. oil in the pan. Sauté beans in oil with the ginger mince and brandy 2-3 minutes. Blend 2 tsp. corn flour in the water and pour over beans. Cook for 2 minutes stirring continuously. Lay fish gently over beans. Add soya sauce. Cover and cook another 2-3 minutes. Uncover and sprinkle spring onions. Cover, cook another 2 minutes. Serve sprinkled with crumbled crisply fried bacon over it, if desired.

Variations

1. Instead of ginger, use 1 tsp. (more or less, according to taste) minced garlic.
2. Can use 4 oz. of canned black beans, in which case no need to steam. Use the water from the can to mix with the corn flour or ½ can and ½ plain water. Reduce salt as often the canned juice could be salty.

LOBSTER IN WINE SAUCE

This is a delicious and easy way to serve lobster, crayfish, or large prawns, given to me by my Chinese friend. Smaller sized prawns may be used but the outcome will never be the same.

Method

Brush lobster (2), crayfish (4-6), prawns (1 kg.) liberally with oil, then broil under the grill or on charcoal. When ready, remove shells, head, and cut into large chunks. If using smaller prawns, should be left whole. (Use your discretion on the chunk size).

Serve with the following sauce poured over:

1" fresh ginger finely sliced	1 tblsp. light soy sauce
3-4 cloves garlic	1 tsp. sesame oil
2 bouillon cubes	2 cups water
2 tblsp. corn starch	1 tblsp. Brandy

Fry ginger and garlic in oil. Add rest of the ingredients except corn starch and brandy. Bring to boil. Let boil for 2-3 minutes. Thicken with corn starch. Just before serving add brandy and pour over sea food.

Serve with plain boiled rice and Chinese cucumber salad (See 'Vegetable' section of the book)

MALAYSIAN SWEET & SOUR PRAWNS OR LOBSTERS (MESAH PEDAS)

Unlike the two previous recipes this is basically a prawn recipe. However, you can also use lobsters, Cray fish or even crabs! In the case of the latter three, either broil as suggested previously, or cook in boiling hot water till colour changes — 15-20 minutes.

1 kg. prawns - clean by removing head, shell, and black thread.

2-4 tbsp. oil.

Sauté in a heavy bottomed fry pan till colour changes and prawns are cooked.

Method

Sauté prawns in a heavy bottomed fry pan till colour changes and prawns are cooked.

Sauce:

3 large onions finely minced	1 tblsp. oil
2-3 red chilli, powder or, cayenne (according to taste)	2 bouillon cubes
2 tblsp. jaggery (grated fine) or brown sugar	2 tblsp. tamarind juice
2 tblsp. finely grated coconut	1½-2 cups of water

Fry onions in oil on low heat till very dark brown. Add chilli powder. Stir well to mix. Add rest of the ingredients and continue to stir till done. This sauce is rather thick. (If necessary, thicken with 1 tbsp. of corn flour). Pour over prawns and blend well with a wooden spoon. Serve with boiled or fried rice or boiled and sautéed noodles.

Variation

Can add fresh or canned ½ cup freshly chopped pineapple to the sauce with the tamarind. Increase or decrease jaggery according to the sweetness of the pineapple. If using canned pineapple use some of the liquid (to taste) to flavour the sauce. Juice oozing out of the fresh pineapple may also be added.

GARLIC & CHILLI PRAWN

(This can be as hot as you like it.)

2-3 tblsp. oil	1 tsp, ginger paste
500 gm. headless prawns, shelled, deveined, and cleaned	2-3 tsp. garlic paste (depends on how garlicky you want it)
1 tsp. cumin powder	1 tsp. sugar
1 tsp. turmeric	4 green chillis (or as many as you like)
250 gm. blanched and chopped tomatoes or, 4 tblsp. tomato purée	2 tblsp. vinegar (or more depending on the number of chillis used

Method

Heat oil. Put in all the spices. Fry well. Add prawns, tomatoes or purée, salt to taste and whole or ground green chilies. Mix all well and bring to boil. Add a little more water if required. Lower heat and simmer till done. When ready, add vinegar, sugar. Stir, take off heat and serve with rice. It should be a nice red colour.

Variations

You can omit the ginger and cumin. Instead sprinkle with cumin powder, when ready before serving.

SWEET & SOUR PRAWN BALLS

Prawn Balls:

8 oz. shrimps/prawns without heads	1-2 tblsp. corn flour
1-2 tblsp. flour	Salt and pepper to taste
1 egg white slightly beaten	¼ cup peanut/sesame oil

Sauce:

1 tblsp. light soy sauce	1 tblsp. red vinegar
1 tblsp. brown sugar	Salt to taste if only the soy sauce is not too salty
1 tblsp. ketchup	1 cup chicken stock
2 tblsp. sherry/brandy (optional)	Freshly ground black pepper to taste
2 tblsp. peanut/sesame oil, if required	1 large onion sliced thickly
2 bunches of spring onions cut in 1" strips	1 tblsp. corn flour

Method

Mince the shrimps or put into the food processor. Add the rest of the ingredients except the oil and form into small balls. Heat oil and fry the balls. Drain on paper towel and keep aside.

Pour off excess oil leaving 2 tblsp in the pan. Mix all the ingredients for the sauce except corn flour and stock in a bowl. Heat oil. Add the onion and cook till transparent. Add the spring onions and stir fry for 1 minute. Pour the mixture from the bowl, stir, and then add the stock. Let all come to a boil, lower heat, and drop the shrimp balls gently into the sauce. Simmer for 2-3 minutes. Before taking off the heat thicken with a paste of the corn flour and 2 tblsp water. Stir for 1 min before removing from heat. Do not let any lumps form in the sauce. (Alternately pour the sauce over the shrimp balls in a dish.) Serve with fried rice or Chinese noodles.

CRAB CASSEROLE

2 small cans (250 gm.) asparagus	2 small cans (250 gm.) crabs
1½ cups long grain rice	1 tblsp. margarine or butter
1 bouillon cube	3 cups water
A little curry powder	Salt and pepper (paprika may be substituted) according to taste

Method

Drain the asparagus and crab and put aside. Put all the above ingredients with the crab and asparagus juice in a saucepan and cook till rice is done. Additional water, bouillon cube and margarine maybe required for extra flavour. Cook till rice is done – should not be too dry or mushy. The rice should be cooked but remain moist.

In a greased casserole arrange in alternate layers rice, crab meat and asparagus. The top and bottom layers should be rice. Pour the following sauce over the casserole. Cover with lid to cover the top. Bake in moderate oven (350 F) for 20/25 minutes.

Sauce:

1 cup mayonnaise	1 egg yolk
1 tblsp. corn starch	1 whipped egg white

Mix all well till well blended.

Serve with melted butter and any kind of salad. A tomato salad with the following dressing goes well. Mix and pour – 1 part vinegar (wine vinegar preferable), 3 parts extra virgin olive, salt and pepper over quartered tomatoes mixed with chopped chives.

STUFFED CRAB

1 tblsp. sesame oil

250 gm. mince from fillet steak

1 bunch spring onion finely minced

1 tblsp. sherry or brandy

2 or more egg yolks

2 large onions finely minced

500 gm. cooked crab meat

1 tblsp. soy sauce

Salt and pepper to taste

Crab shells

Method

Heat oil, fry onions lightly. Add mince and continue frying till colour changes. Now add the crab, spring onions, and stir well. Add all the other ingredients except egg yolks. Cook all together, till well mixed. Take off heat and bind with egg yolks. Fill shells, which have been previously washed and dried, with mixture. Drizzle with butter generously. Place filled shells on a baking sheet and bake in a moderate to hot oven (375^0F) till filling shrinks from the side.

Variations:

Instead of crab shells the above mixture may be used to fill individual oven proof scallop bowls or egg plants. In the case of the latter, halve large eggplants in two. Take out all the pulp from the halves. Fill with crab mixture, sprinkle breadcrumbs on top, dot with butter and bake till top is golden brown.

Steam or roast the eggplant pulp. Mash well preferably in the food processor till smooth. Mix with a little olive oil, minced onion or a little garlic powder, salt & pepper and paprika. Serve as an accompaniment to any main course or as a dip for salted crackers or cut vegetables e.g. carrots, cucumber etc. etc.

BAKED CRAB

4 large crabs cooked	2 tblsp. butter or, sesame oil
2-3 smoked or Chinese sausages (optional)	1 bunch spring onions finely chopped
1 celery stick finely chopped	1 tblsp. cooked tender green peas
1 small green or red capsicum deseeded and chopped	2 tsp. light soy sauce
6-8 medium mushrooms chopped	Salt and black pepper to taste
A pinch of *ajinomoto*	1 tblsp. Corn flour or, 1 egg
Chilli sauce (optional) to taste	1-2 tblsp. fine breadcrumbs

Method

Break the claws from the main body of the crab. Crack them and take out the flesh. Now crack the shell in half. Take out the meat and coral. Discard all the rest – green and black parts. Reserve the top half of the shell for the filling. Break the crabmeat with a fork. In 1 tblsp oil cook the sausage meat breaking it into small bits resembling ground meat. Keep aside. In the same pan sauté the rest of the ingredients in 1 tblsp oil excluding the peas, sauces, seasonings, corn flour and breadcrumbs for about 2-3 minutes. Take off heat and mix with the crabmeat. Add all the rest of the ingredients except corn flour, breadcrumbs, and oil. Mix till well blended. Finally add the corn flour to bind. If mixture is too dry, make a paste of the corn flour with 4 tblsp water before adding. Alternately 1 egg may also be added. Stuff the crab shells with the filling. Lightly sprinkle the top of each shell with breadcrumbs to cover. Dot with the remaining oil or butter. Bake in a moderate oven till top is well browned. This can be served as a starter before the main meal accompanied with a green or tomato salad.

Crab meat is often sold cooked and dressed. All one has to do is to ask for the shells

----

FISH BROWN STEW

500 gm. (6-8 pcs.) good fish with minimum bones cut in serving pieces

3 potatoes quartered

Salt and pepper to taste

3-4 tblsp. oil

1" pc. Cinnamon

2-3 whole black pepper corns

3-4 medium tomatoes chopped

3-4 medium cabbage leaves

4-5 baby carrots scraped and left whole or 3-4 medium carrots scraped and cut in thick slices in ½" lengths

1 bay leaf

4 cloves

2 green cardamoms

1 large onion sliced

4 small whole onions peeled

4-6 thin slices of fresh ginger

2 cups or more water

Method

Rub fish pieces with salt and keep aside for 10-15 minutes. Heat oil in a saucepan. Brown potatoes and carrots slightly and keep aside. Add 1 tblsp oil to the pan only if necessary. Put in bay leaf, cloves, cinnamon, cardamom, and whole pepper corns. When they start to splutter add the sliced onion and brown. Add the chopped tomatoes and cook for a few minutes or till they are soft. Add all the other ingredients except the fish and chillis. Mix all well together and cook for 2 minutes. Add water and let come to boil. Lower heat, cover and cook till vegetables are done. Now add the fish and chillis and cook for another 5 minutes. Be careful not to let the fish disintegrate. Serve with rice.

Variations:

1. Instead of chopped tomatoes use 1-2 tblsp tomato paste or purée. Add this after browning the onions with the vegetables.
2. Instead of adding chopped tomatoes at the beginning they could be added with the water.
3. Omit the tomatoes totally. Use minimum oil. Just before taking stew off the heat add 1 tblsp butter or margarine.
4. Chicken or mutton may also be made in any of the above ways.

FISH WHITE STEW

500 gm. fish with less bones cut in serving pieces	Salt and pepper to taste
1 bay leaf	4 cloves
4 whole black pepper corns	3-4 slices ginger
2 large potatoes peeled and cut in thick round slices	4-6 baby carrots or 3 whole medium carrots scraped and cut in ½" lengths
4-6 onions peeled and left whole	1 tblsp. flour
1 tblsp. milk	2 tblsp. butter or margarine
2-3 sprigs of parsley for garnish	1-2 cups of water

Method

Rub fish pieces with salt and keep aside. Heat the water in a saucepan with the bay leaf, cloves, peppercorns, and ginger slices. When it comes to the boil add all the vegetables except the onions. Cover and cook till the vegetables are almost done. Reduce heat and add the whole onions and then the fish pieces. Add salt and pepper. Cook till onions are soft and the fish is done. Mix flour and milk together and gradually pour into the stew stirring constantly to avoid lumps from forming. When the stew becomes smooth and begins to thicken add the butter. Take off heat and serve surrounded by plain boiled rice or boiled rice and green peas mixed together.

Variations:

Instead of putting all the spices in water at the beginning heat 1-2 tsp oil. Add the spices and when they start spluttering add all the vegetables except onions. Cook for about 2-3 minutes. Add water, cover, cook and continue as above.

STELLAMASHI'S HILSA PĀRĀ (PICKLED HILSA)

2-3 lbs. hilsa (or shad)

A pinch of saltpetre

2-4 tblsp. oil for frying

2 tblsp vinegar (approx.)

1-2 tsp. salt

8 oz. tamarind (4 oz. tamarind to every lb. of. fish)

2 or more large onions sliced

Method

Cut fish in serving pieces. Omit the oily parts. Wash and dry completely with paper towel. There should be no water adhering to the fish. Rub salt and very little ground saltpetre on both sides of the fish. Soak tamarind in just enough vinegar to cover for ½ hr. Grind to a paste. Marinate fish in this for 2 to 3 days. If saltpetre is used it may be kept outside otherwise it is safer to keep in the refrigerator. After 3 days all the fine bones and most of the tough bones should dissolve.

Heat oil. Fry sliced onions brown. Add the fish pieces and cook a little more till done. Serve with potato julienne, boiled or fried rice and a salad. Can also be served on toast as a snack. Slightly mashed makes a good filling for crepes.

SMOKED HILSA - THE EASY WAY

1 kg. hilsa (or shad) fillet	2-4 tblsp. oil
2-3 tsp. anchovy or, any fish sauce	1 tblsp. ketchup
1-2 tblsp. Worcester sauce	1-2 tblsp. red, white, or wine vinegar
½ tsp. paprika	Salt and pepper to taste
1-2 tblsp. or more 'smoke oil (preferably hickory).	A little red colouring *'ratanjote'* or substitute

Method

Marinate the fillets in the above mixture for 5-6 hrs. Next place on a greased baking sheet and cook in a moderately hot oven till fish is done. Remove from oven. Hold each fillet down with a fork or knife and pull the bones out from the centre gradually and carefully with another knife keeping the fish whole. Once the bones are taken out from one side, turn the fillet and take the bones out from the other side in a similar way. De-bone all the fillets in this way. After cooking most of the bones should have become soft or melted so, de-boning should not be a difficult task. Carefully transfer the fish to a flat serving dish. Sprinkle top with crisply fried grated potatoes. Garnish with lemon wedges.

COLD HERRING SWEDISH STYLE

2 salted herrings

1 medium onion sliced

1 medium carrot sliced thinly

5 whole Allspice

¾ cup sugar

½ leek sliced thinly

1 bay leaf

¼ cup white vinegar

1 cup water

Method

Soak herrings in cold water overnight. Change water several times to get the salt out. Pat herrings dry and clean by peeling the skin off. Do not take out the bones. Cut the fish diagonally in small pieces and mix with the vegetables and spices. Arrange on a serving platter.

Boil vinegar, sugar, and water till sugar dissolves and all well blended. Cool. pour over herrings. Serve with rye or any other brown or dark bread. Herrings may be placed on a bed of lettuce surrounded by slices of boiled potatoes, eggs, and slices of tomato.

FRIED PRAWNS

1 lb. prawns shelled and minus heads	1 tblsp. each onion and ginger paste
1 tblsp. vinegar or, fresh lime juice	1-2 eggs slightly beaten
1-2 dash tblsp. water	½ cup dry shifted flour
1 cup (more or less) breadcrumbs	1-2 cups oil for frying
Salt and pepper or, paprika to taste	

Method

De-vein prawns, wash, pat dry on paper towel. Marinate for several hours in the spices, vinegar, and seasoning. Take out and shake off all excess marinade from the prawns. On a wooden board flatten each prawn with the back of a wooden spoon to make it big. Be careful not to tear the prawn by beating too much. Mix the eggs with the water. Dust each prawn in the flour. Shake off excess. Rest for 5-10 minutes. Now dip each prawn in the egg mixture and then roll in the breadcrumbs. Repeat the egg and crumb process once more. Again, let rest for about half an hour. Heat oil and deep fry the prawn cutlets carefully. Drain on paper towel. Arrange on a flat serving dish surrounded with potato chips or crisps, lemon wedges grated lemon and/or cucumber. Mayonnaise or tartar sauce and/or ketchup make good accompaniments. Alternately mix 1 cup ketchup with 1 tblsp French mustard and 2 tsp wine or plain vinegar. If the prawns are large this could be served as a main course. It can also be served as a cocktail snack. If the prawns are small, several can be added and beaten together to enlarge each cutlet to the required size.

TEMPURA (I)

(Tempura can be served as a first course at a dinner or as a cocktail or tea-time snack. It is basically either prawns, fish fillets or vegetables coated in a light batter, deep fried and served immediately with a sauce.)

Shrimps -	Minus the heads. Take out the black thread, turn over and make a few cuts across
Fish -	Small thin fillets, the size of a finger
Carrots -	Shredded into finger lengths
Green beans -	Thin slices or strings cut across the grain
Brinjals & onions -	Thin round slices the size of a canapé
Green or red pepper -	De-seeded and cut as above
Radish -	1 cup finely grated or ground
Salt & ajinomoto -	Mixed to taste
Oil -	For frying

Batter:

2 egg yolks	1 cup ice water
1 cup flour sifted	

Method

Mix the batter ingredients lightly with a wooden spoon. Do not beat. Spread some flour on a plate. Always cook the shrimps and fish first. Pick the items up preferably with chop sticks or wooden tongs, roll in the plate of flour, dip in the batter then fry in hot oil. Drain on paper towels and serve hot accompanied with a mixture of salt and ajinomoto and tempura sauce, or a mixture of finely grated radish and tempura sauce.

Fish should be done and served the same way as the shrimps.

The vegetables should be fried in small bunches stuck with a toothpick if necessary and removed later. The vegetables do not have to be rolled in the dry flour. If liked a combination of similar type of vegetables like carrots and perhaps green beans could be bunched together.

Tempura Sauce:

2 cups stock preferably chicken or from bouillon cubes

½ cup soy sauce preferably Japanese

1/3 cup sake or any white wine

Mix all together well without beating and serve.

Variation:

Thin slices of pork or beef fillet or thin slices of chicken breast can also be cooked this way. The size should be kept small and proportionate.

TEMPURA (II)

1 egg	1 cup cold water
1 cup or more flour sifted	½-1 cup oil for deep frying
½ lb. headless shrimps with tails cleaned or, thin strips of fish	1 medium carrot cut in julienne strips
1-2 medium onions sliced thin	1 green pepper cut into strips or squires
4-5 green beans cut in julienne strips	Soy sauce

Method

Mix the egg with the water lightly without beating. Add the flour lightly and quickly. Heat the oil. Coat the shrimps in the mixture leaving the tail free and deep fry. If using fish, coat similarly before frying. Fry all the other vegetables after coating in the mixture. The very thinly cut vegetables can be coated in bunches and fried. The hard-skinned vegetables like green pepper should be coated and fried separately. The soft skinned vegetables may be coated and fried in individual or mixed bunches e.g. carrots and green beans. Serve hot with a small bowl of soy sauce separately. The tempura is dipped in soy sauce before eating. Lemon juice, salt & pepper may be sprinkled over the tempura and served in which case, omit the soy sauce.

Alternately the following sauce can also be served with the tempura:

A mixture of Japanese stock or bouillon cube, sake, soy sauce and grated radish – the amount of each ingredient depends on individual taste.

MUMMY'S MASALA (OR SPICY) FISH

1 Kg. of a whole fish, fish fillets, or cut pieces of fish

Marinade:

2 heaped tblsp. or more of freshly ground onions	½ tsp. garam masala (equal mixture of powdered cinnamon, cloves, and cardamom) made into a paste with a little bit of water
2 heaped tsp. freshly ground ginger	2 heaped tsp. freshly ground garlic
1 tsp. coriander powder	1 tsp. cumin powder
2 tblsp. oil	

Fish:

1-2 bay leaves	1 tblsp. red wine vinegar (if no available, white vinegar will suffice)
Salt to taste	Green or red chillis to taste
5-6 raisins	1 tblsp. freshly chopped coriander leaves

Method

Marinate 1 whole fish, fish fillet, or cut pieces of fish in the following marinade:

Marinade:

Plenty of onion, ginger, garlic, cummin, coriander, a small amount of cinnamon. cloves and cardamom paste. Add a fair amount of oil to the fish and let rest for ½ to 1 hr. or so.

Fish:

In a large fry pan lay fish without letting the cut pieces overlap. Place 1 or 2 bay leaves on top of the fish. Cook on low heat covered. Gradually raise heat to medium and uncover. Cook till there's a thick gravy. Turn off heat. In a small bowl add 1 tblsp red or wine vinegar, salt, green or red chillis if desired, and a few raisins. Stir and pour over the fish. Turn on heat for a few seconds. Sprinkle chopped coriander leaves on top. Serve with plain boiled rice.

STUFFED FISH

Approximately 2 Kg. of a whole fish or larger

Chopped plain or smoked ham – sufficient to stuff the fish

½ cup soy sauce

2 tblsp. sugar

2 heaped tsp. freshly ground ginger

2 heaped tsp. freshly ground garlic

2 tblsp. oil or more, as required

Method

Use a fairly large whole fish. If desired, carefully remove the centre bone. Stuff fish with chopped plain or smoked ham. Stitch the side to prevent it from opening.

In a bowl, mix soy sauce, ground ginger, garlic, sugar, and oil. Rub this mixture well on the fish. Place in a medium hot oven and cook till done and fish is a golden colour.

POULTRY

CHICKEN WITH ORANGES

2 large chickens (approx. 1.5 kg. each) skinned and cut in serving pieces

2 tblsp. flour

¼ tsp. ground cloves

1-2 orange sections

¼ tsp. salt

¼ tsp. Tabasco sauce

1½ cup orange juice (1 cup fresh juice & ½ cup water or ½ 'Tang" & ½ water)

1/3 tsp. ground cinnamon

1/3 cup raisins

½ cup almonds finely chopped

4 tblsp. butter

Method

Rub chicken in salt and brown in butter. Remove and keep aside. To the pan juices add flour, salt and all the spices. Stir till smooth and thick but not too pasty. Add orange juice and Tabasco sauce. Cook stirring constantly till it starts to boil and is thick. Add chicken pieces with the almonds and raisins. Cover and simmer on low heat till chicken pieces are tender. Just before taking off the heat add the orange segments and let cook slowly for another 5 minutes to incorporate the flavour of orange into the dish. Remove to a serving platter and serve surrounded by boiled rice and peas. Can garnish with a few mint leaves.

CURRIED ORANGE CHICKEN

1 medium chicken (approx. 1-1.2 kg, cut into serving pieces with skin on.

1 tblsp. honey

½ cup or a little more orange juice

Salt to taste

2 tblsp. cold water

¼ tsp. freshly ground black pepper or paprika (optional)

1-2 tsp. curry powder

2 tblsp. dry mustard

1 tblsp. corn flour

Method

Sprinkle chicken with curry powder and arrange in a baking dish. Do not let chicken pieces overlap.

In a saucepan simmer ¼ cup orange juice, honey and mustard till well blended. Add salt and pepper or paprika if using. Pour the sauce over the chicken and bake in a moderately hot oven for about ½ hr. Turn chicken and continue baking for another 20 minutes or till chicken is tender. Place chicken on a serving dish. Combine corn flour, cold water and the pan juices and scrapings from the tray where the chicken was cooked. Cook on medium heat stirring all the time till it comes to the boil and starts bubbling. Lower heat and add the rest of the orange juice. Cook another 2 minutes till all well blended. Pour this over the chicken in the serving dish or serve separately as a sauce accompanied with a mixture of plain boiled rice and peas. Can serve the peas separately tossed in a little butter and coated with chopped parsley or coriander leaves.

TOMATO CHICKEN

1-2 tbsp. (or more depending on the strength) tomato purée

2 cups water

1 large or 2 small bay leaves

1-1½ kg. chicken skinned and cut up in large serving pieces

Salt and pepper to taste

1-2 bouillon cubes crumbled

1 tblsp. olive oil

5-6 cloves garlic peeled

1 tblsp. oregano or Italian seasoning

Method

In a bowl prepare ready a mixture of tomato puree, bouillon cubes, salt, pepper, and the water. Heat oil slightly in a large flat heavy bottomed or non-stick pan. Add the bay leaf. After a minute add the whole garlic cloves. Stir constantly for 1 minute. Do not let it burn. Now place the chicken pieces carefully in the pan. Cook stirring and turning frequently till the chicken pieces turn white. Make sure they do not stick to the pan. Pour the tomato puree mixture over the chicken. Add the oregano or Italian seasoning. Cook till chicken is done. If necessary, add a little more warm water. The dish should not have too much liquid. There should be a thick gravy just halfway up the chicken or just enough to cover with the chicken visible. Serve surrounded by a ring of steamed rice or spaghetti. Sprinkle with parmesan cheese. Garnish with sprigs of parsley. Serve extra parmesan in a bowl. A tomato or green salad is a good accompaniment.

Variations:

Fish or meatballs may be made in the same way. If using fish, sprinkle a 250 gm. fish fillet cut into 6-8 serving pieces with salt and sauté in a little olive oil. Keep aside. Proceed with the sauce as above. Let it come to the boil. Lower heat and let simmer for 5 minutes. Place the fish gently into the sauce. Continue cooking till sauce is thick and penetrates the fish. The fish should not break. Now serve as above.

Meat Balls:

Use any ground meat – about 250 gm. Combine with 2 tsp finely minced capsicum, 1 tsp finely minced parsley, 1-2 tsp cornflour to bind and 1 tsp garlic powder if desired. Make into small balls and shallow fry till brown in olive oil.

When the sauce comes to boil drop the meat balls into it and reduce heat. Cook till the sauce penetrates the meat balls. Now serve as above.

Instead of tomato puree 1 cup or more tomatoes blanched, peeled, and mashed may be substituted. A combination of tomato puree and fresh tomatoes may also be used. However, if tomatoes are being used, they should be red and ripe.

QUICK SPICY CHICKEN

1 kg. chicken skinned and cut into medium serving pieces	2 tblsp. onion paste
1 tblsp. garlic paste	1 tblsp. ginger paste
4 tblsp. oil	3-4 bay leaves
1 tblsp. raisins (optional)	2-3 fresh whole green chillis de-seeded and split but kept whole
2 tsp. almonds slivered thinly (optional)	½ cup water
Salt and pepper to taste	

Method

Mix the chicken pieces with salt, pepper, onion, garlic, and ginger pastes. Leave to rest in the marinade for about 2 hours - this brings out the flavour better. However, if time is short the chicken may be cooked immediately. Warm oil, preferably in a pressure cooker. Add the bay leaves. When they begin to splutter add the chicken pieces with all the juices. Turn chicken constantly while cooking – it should not get brown. When the spices are fried and done add the water, green chillis, cover and pressure cook for 10-25 minutes depending on the tenderness of the chicken. Uncover pressure cooker and add the raisins. Keep uncovered on heat to dry off excess liquid. This dish should be white and dryish with the oil floating on top. Add the almonds (if using) and stir, just before taking off the heat.

Serve with small whole peeled potatoes cooked with the chicken or just boiled creamed and mashed, steamed parsley coated green peas or a mixture of green beans cut small, cubed carrots, cauliflower cut small and peas. Plain boiled rice or vegetable fried rice are also good accompaniments.

Variations:

This chicken may also be cooked in the oven. Lay the chicken pieces in an oven proof dish with all the spices, bay leaves green chillis and oil. No water to be added as enough water will come out from the chicken. Cover and cook in a medium hot oven. Turn chicken pieces over once or twice if required.

When chicken is done uncover and dry off excess liquid in the oven. This will take about 1 hour to 1½ hours.

The same method can be used to cook in the microwave. Cook on power level 7 for about 15 - 20 minutes.

This can also be cooked in a heavy -bottomed wide pan instead of the pressure cooker. This will of course take much longer to cook. In this method care should be taken to see that it does not stick and get burnt at the bottom.

PIQUANT CHICKEN

1 kg. chicken with skin

1" piece ginger sliced thin

2 tblsp. brown sugar or honey

1 tsp. tamarind paste

1½ cup water

1 whole bulb garlic minced fine

1 tblsp. dark soy sauce

¼ tsp. aniseed powder

1-2 tblsp. oil

Salt and pepper to taste

Method

Mix all the above ingredients together except chicken. Bring mixture to boil, lower heat, and simmer till all well blended. Add the whole chicken and cook on low heat covered till tender and the liquid has reduced considerably. There should be just enough liquid to coat the chicken. Serve the chicken whole with the thick gravy and Chinese vegetable fried rice. If preferred the chicken can also be cut in large serving pieces after it has been cooked. Alternatively, just before serving take chicken out of the gravy and brown under the grill or broiler and serve whole or cut in pieces with the gravy poured over it.

CHICKEN WITH SWEET HOT SAUCE

1 small chicken bouillon cube	½-¾ cup hot water
2 tsp. liquid jaggery ('*nolen goor*')/honey/treacle	2 tblsp. orange/peach/lichi juice
2 tsp. garlic powder	1 tsp. ginger powder
½ tsp. hot paprika/chilli powder	1 tblsp. dark soy sauce (optional)
4 chicken breasts de-boned	2 tblsp. flour
Salt and pepper to taste	2 tblsp. butter/margarine
2 tblsp. oil	A dash of 'angostura' bitters (optional)

Method

Dissolve bouillon cube in the hot water. Stir in the fruit juice, jaggery or substitute, bitters, garlic, ginger powder and paprika. Blend well and keep aside till required. This is the sauce.

Flatten the chicken breasts with a mallet or back of a knife gently without damaging the meat. Now dust the breasts in the flour seasoned with salt & pepper. Melt the butter over low heat and then add the oil and stir to mix. Fry the chicken on both sides a golden brown. Pour the sauce over the chicken and cook covered till chicken is almost done. Remove cover and cook some more. There should be very little liquid. Place on a flat dish surrounded with a border of mashed potatoes which has been browned slightly golden under the grill. Garnish with a combination of grated carrot, radish, and cabbage (both red and green can be mixed for added colour).

Note: Angostura bitters can be substituted by gin or vodka.

CHICKEN COGNAC

2 lb. tender chicken with skin, cut in serving pieces

1 cup cognac (more or less)

Salt and pepper to taste

4 oz. (or more) butter

1 cup (more or less) water

Method

Smear the chicken pieces with salt & pepper. Melt butter on low heat and fry chicken slowly till slightly brown turning frequently. Pour cognac over the chicken and continue frying a little more or till chicken almost done. Always cook slowly on low heat making sure not to burn the chicken. Add the water and cook till the chicken is fully done. All the water should disappear with only the butter remaining. This is a delicious dish if done properly. Serve with mashed, braised, or fried potatoes and a green salad.

In the absence of cognac use any other brandy though the former has the best results flavour-wise.

CHEESY CHICKEN WITH SOUR CREAM

8 oz. (or more) butter/olive oil

8 oz. (or more) button mushrooms preferably canned

A pinch of paprika (optional)

1 cup water

4 oz. sour cream sauce

1 large onion chopped

1 chicken (approx. 2 lb.) cut in serving pieces

Salt and pepper to taste

8 oz. cheese sauce

Method

Heat butter or olive oil and fry the onion. Remove and drain on paper towel. Sauté the mushrooms and keep aside. Add some more oil if necessary and fry the chicken pieces till golden brown. Add the already fried onions and mushroom. At this time add the paprika if using and the salt & pepper. Mix all well. Add the water and simmer till chicken is done. Alternately pressure cook for 10-15 minutes. While chicken is still hot pour hot cheese sauce over it and stir. Just before serving add the sour cream and stir. The chicken should be warm and not too hot. The sour cream should be of room temperature. It is better not to heat the chicken after adding the sour cream.

Cheese Sauce:

1 tblsp. heaped butter

Salt and pepper to taste

1 cup milk

1 small onion minced

1 tblsp flour sifted

½ cup mild cheese grated

Melt butter on low heat. Add the onion and flour and stir to mix with a wooden ladle. Add the milk gradually and keep stirring till sauce begins to thicken. Add the seasoning and cheese. Mix all well – there should be no lumps.

Sour Cream Sauce:

4 oz. cream

½ tsp. mixed herb or fresh dill minced

1 tblsp. heaped yogurt unsweetened

Mix all well and keep aside for ½ hour or so. The sour cream should be smooth and not have a curdled appearance.

Sour cream as well. In the absence of these the above methods can be used successfully, as sour cream and cheese sauce with instructions are available off the shelf. Add the herbs to the plain sour cream

Serve with boiled rice, with peas and carrot cubes, mixed and a green salad.

PIQUANT CHICKEN STEW

1.5-2 kg. chicken cut in serving pieces	2 tblsp. chopped spring onions
2 tblsp. sesame or peanut oil	4 tblsp. light soy sauce
1 tblsp paprika	1 tblsp. garlic minced
1 tsp. gourmet powder (monosodium glutamate) or a bouillon cube	Salt and pepper to taste
	4 tblsp. water

Method

Mix all the above ingredients except the water and keep aside for 1-2 hours. Put chicken in an ovenproof dish with a cover. Add the water only if there is not sufficient liquid. Cover and cook in a medium low oven for 1 ½ hrs or till chicken done. Serve on a platter surrounded by boiled rice. This dish may also be cooked in the microwave on low power in which case it will take half the time of cooking. Alternately this stew could be cooked on top of the stove on very low heat. Check from time to time and stir so that it does not stick in the bottom. if cooked on top of the stove it may require a little more liquid.

Variations:

1. Omit the garlic and substitute 1 tblsp chopped ginger. Instead of ground pepper use 4-5 whole black or green peppercorns.
2. Beef or lamb may be cooked as the above.

GROUNDNUT STEW

(The following recipe is from Ghana. It is traditionally cooked with chicken, but other meats or hard vegetables may be substituted. Slow cooking is recommended for this recipe to bring out the best flavour which is unfortunately time consuming. However, the ground nut stew tastes the best with chicken and the time spent over the cooking is worthwhile.)

Peanut Sauce:

2 jars chunky peanut butter (approx. 360 gm. each)	2 peanut jars of water + 4 pts. of water
	+ 1 pt. water
1 tsp. salt	2 tblsp. onion chopped

Chicken Soup:

2 large chickens (approx. 2 kg each) cut into serving pieces	2 tblsp. onions chopped + 180 gm onion chopped
Oil for frying	1-2 cloves garlic
Salt and black pepper to taste	

Tomato Juice:

4 large tomatoes	Hot water
½ tblsp. ginger paste	1 small bay leaf
A pinch of rosemary	Chilli powder to taste

Method

*Peanut Sauce***:**

Cook all the ingredients with the first portion of water on low heat stirring occasionally to prevent sticking. Keep cooking till the oil from the peanut butter floats to the top. Add the second portion of water, mix well and strain through a soup strainer. Add the third portion of the water to the saucepan scraping bottom and sides well. Add to the sauce and stir well.

Chicken Soup:

Cook the chicken in it's own juice with the garlic and the first portion of the onions, salt & pepper. (All the parts of the chicken e.g. liver, gizzard etc. can be used). When the chicken is done, take out of the pan, drain, dry and then fry the pieces in a little oil. Return to the pan with the juices and add the second portion of the onions.

Tomato Juice:

Cover the tomatoes with hot water. Let rest for 5-10 minutes. Put through a food processor or a blender

Final Assembly:

Put the peanut sauce back on heat. Add the chicken mixture. Add the tomato juice with the ginger and all the other ingredients. Cook without covering for ½ hr, lower heat, and simmer for another ½ hour. The stew should be thick. If the chicken is very tough add to the soup at the very beginning. If chicken is tender, then add ½ hr before the stew is ready but make sure to add the chicken stock with the spices to the stew from the beginning. Serve with boiled rice and all the accompaniments of an Indian curry e.g. grated coconut, minced onions, chutneys, pickles, *raitas* etc. etc.

If the stew is to be served as a soup, then keep it light by increasing the water and lessening the spices according to the requirement. The longer the chicken is in the stew the better the taste.

SAVOURY CAKE WITH CHICKEN FILLING

Dough:

5 eggs	2 tblsp. (or less) sugar
4 oz. flour	½ tsp. (or more) salt

Filling:

1 tblsp. oil	4 oz. boneless chicken boiled and cut small
4 oz. shrimps	2 medium onions chopped
4 oz. smoked tongue chopped	¼ cup milk
1-2 tblsp. flour	Salt and pepper to taste
¼ cup water	1 tblsp. celery and/or capsicum minced
¼ tsp. nutmeg grated	

Method

Make the dough by putting the eggs and sugar in the food processor. Sift the flour and salt together and add to the egg mixture. Mix well.

To make the filling heat the oil and fry the chicken, shrimps, and tongue with the onions till light brown. Add the flour, milk, water, seasoning, nutmeg, and celery. Stir to mix. Cook till mixture begins to thicken. Take off the heat.

Grease and flour muffin tins or use paper cups for cupcakes. Put 1 tblsp of dough in the tin/cup. Put sufficient filling and cover with another tablespoon of dough. Bake in a hot oven for 15-20 minutes. If using muffin tins loosen sides and cool on a wire tray before taking out. For paper cups just cool on wire tray.

STUFFED ROAST CHICKEN

1 large (3-5 lb.) chicken with skin and insides intact, dressed, and ready for the oven	1 large can (approx. 8 oz.) mushrooms chopped
½ litre or less milk	10-12 oz. butter
1 tblsp. heaped parsley chopped	4 large slices of bread
5 eggs	2 cups water
Salt, pepper, and allspice to taste	

Method

Roughly chop the insides of the chicken – liver, heart, and gizzard. Soak the bread in the milk. Melt 6 oz. butter in a pan. Fry the chicken liver etc and keep stirring. Put the bread in a strainer or colander and squeeze out all the excess milk with the back of a wooden spoon. When the liver etc. is browned add the bread. Stir and cook for a few minutes. Add the parsley and mushrooms. Add salt, pepper and allspice. Now add the eggs one by one stirring continuously till the butter is absorbed and the mixture is fairly dry. Cool and stuff the chicken from the stomach opening. Sew the neck with thread so that the stuffing does not escape. Stitch the stomach opening also after the stuffing is in. Sprinkle chicken with salt and pepper. Take a large pat of butter and put on the roasting pan. Stick a few lumps of butter on the chicken also. Add the water to the roasting pan. Place in a hot oven and cook till chicken is done about 1 hr. Turn from time to time, basting with the pan juices. If desired reduce heat to medium after 15 minutes.

Serve with roast potatoes which may be cooked together with the chicken, surrounding it in the roasting pan or separately. Any vegetable can be served along with it. Halved or quartered whole cabbage steamed is a good accompaniment.

Brown Sauce:

Made from the pan juices also, is a must as an accompaniment. Scrape the pan juices and place in a saucepan. Brown 1-2 tblsp flour and mix with the contents of the saucepan smoothly. Add about 1- 2 cups water and bring to boil stirring continuously. Add seasoning and any browning sauce favoured. Lower heat and simmer till thick. Continue stirring constantly and beat, if necessary, with a wooden spoon so that no lumps form.

CHICKEN & CORN BAKE (I)

1½-2 kg. chicken	4 large corn cobs
2 tblsp. heaped butter	2 tblsp. heaped flour or cornflour/starch
Milk and water as required	1 large onion chopped
6 tblsp. cheddar or substitute grated	4 egg yolks
½ tsp. sweet or hot paprika (optional)	Salt and pepper to taste
1-2 tblsp. breadcrumbs	4 egg whites

Method

Boil the chicken whole in sufficient water, de-bone and cut small. Reserve the liquid. Boil the corn in sufficient water. Take the kernels out and either put in the liquidizer or food processor. Reserve the excess liquid from the boiled corns. Both the chicken and the corns may be pressure- cooked separately making sure they are not over cooked. Make a roux of the butter, flour or corn-starch and onions in a saucepan over medium heat. As soon as the onion turns transparent add the excess liquid from the chicken and corn and enough milk/water to make a fairly thick white sauce. Keep stirring the mixture with a wooden spoon until it begins to thicken. Do not let any lumps form.

Take off heat, cool slightly and add the yolks one at a time beating well after each addition, to blend. Add 4 tblsp grated cheese and stir to mix. Now add the chicken and the corn stirring gently till well mixed. Add salt, pepper and paprika, mix well. Beat egg whites stiff and gently fold into the chicken mixture. Pour into an oven proof dish. Sprinkle the remaining grated cheese on top followed by the breadcrumbs. Dot with butter and bake in a medium hot oven till brown. Serve with any salad of choice.

Note.

400 gm canned corn kernels or 400 gm. creamed corn may be substituted. In this case no need to boil the corn.

CHICKEN & CORN BAKE (II)

3 tblsp. butter	2 tblsp. flour
1 onion chopped	3 cups milk
2-3 egg yolks	4 corn cobs boiled and puréed
1 kg. (approx.) chicken boiled, de-boned and cut small	2-3 egg whites
Salt and pepper to taste	2-3 tblsp. grated cheese (optional)

Method

In a saucepan combine butter, flour and onion and stir over med. heat till all well blended. Reduce heat and add the milk gradually stirring continuously with a wooden spoon until sauce begins to thicken. Take off heat and add the egg yolks one at a time beating after each addition. Now add the corn purée and the chopped chicken and salt and pepper to taste. Also add the cheese if using. Beat egg whites stiff and gently fold into the chicken mixture. Turn into a greased oven proof casserole. Sprinkle top with grated cheddar or parmesan cheese. Bake in a moderately hot oven for about ½ hour or till set. Serve with any salad of choice.

Variations:

1. Canned asparagus spears may be used instead of corn. No need to purée asparagus.
2. Add 1-2 tblsp mayonnaise to the white sauce after taking it off the heat and before adding the egg yolks.

CHICKEN & ASPARAGUS

Method

The same ingredients and method as the "Chicken & Corn Bake" should be used. Substitute the corn with either fresh or canned asparagus. No need to boil the fresh asparagus. Just cut them into small bits. If using canned asparagus, drain the liquid which should be used with the chicken liquid to make the white sauce. No need to cut the asparagus. Lay them in alternate layers with the chicken mixture in the oven proof dish.

BAKED CHICKEN

Method

This dish is made the same way as the "Chicken & Corn Bake" or the "Chicken & Asparagus" without the corn and asparagus. However, for the extra flavor can add 1-2 tblsp spicy tomato juice and 1 tsp prepared mustard. Alternately add ½ cup cream gently to the chicken mixture and bake in a very low oven with the dish placed in a pan of water. 1 tsp cinnamon/clove/mixed spice powder also adds to the flavour. 1-2 tsp curry powder can also be used. If preferred, the cheese could be omitted. As "Baked Chicken" is a very flexible dish any table-sauce, soy sauce or Worcestershire sauce can also be added. All one needs as usual, is some imagination! If cream is not added, then bake in a moderately hot oven. In either case sprinkle top with breadcrumbs and cheese if using.

CHICKEN BAKED WITH GARLIC

2 kg. chicken cut in serving pieces	2-4 tblsp. oil
Salt and pepper to taste	2 large carrots cut in long strips
4 celery sticks cut in long strips	2 large onions cut in strips
40 cloves (or more) garlic peeled	1 large bunch parsley chopped
1 cup dry white vermouth	1-2 tblsp. cognac

Method

Rub the chicken pieces with oil, salt, and pepper. If necessary, steam the chicken - for 1-1½ hours. or half cook before rubbing oil, salt, and pepper. In an oven proof dish with cover lay the chicken, carrot, celery, onion, garlic, and parsley in layers. Pour the vermouth and cognac over the whole. Cover dish with foil and place the lid of the dish over it. Bake in a moderately hot oven for 1 ½ hour or till done. Take the garlic out and mash. Also take the chicken pieces out and de-bone leaving the vegetables in the casserole.

Method of serving: Grill slices of buttered toast or toast on a griddle. Spread the slices with mashed garlic and then top them with chicken pieces. Serve the vegetables separately in the casserole. If this dish is served as a main course a green salad is a good accompaniment.

ITALIAN FLAVOURED BAKED CHICKEN

1 kg. chicken cut in serving pieces	¼ cup or more oil
1 cup button mushrooms	2-3 bay leaves
4-6 cloves garlic	1 cup spicy ketchup
1 tblsp. Italian seasoning/oregano/dried or freshly minced mint leaves	a mixture of dried or freshly chopped parsley and coriander.
1 tsp. hot/sweet paprika	1 cup hot water
2-4 tblsp. any red wine	1 tsp. corn flour (optional)
Salt and pepper to taste	

Top Crust:

1-2 tblsp. butter	1-2 tblsp. milk
Salt and pepper to taste	A pinch of paprika
4-5 potatoes cooked and mashed	

Method

Brown the chicken pieces in the oil. (Omit all pieces which do not have much meat e.g. neck, ribs, wing tips, liver, gizzard etc.) Remove the browned chicken and lay in a baking dish without overlapping. Sauté the mushrooms in a little oil and place over the chicken. Heat 1 tblsp oil. Add the bay leaves and then the garlic cloves whole. When slightly brown add the ketchup, herbs, water, paprika and wine. Let the mixture come to a boil. If the sauce is too thin add the corn flour mixed to a paste with a little cold water. As the sauce begins to thicken take off heat and pour over the chicken. The sauce should not be too thick or too thin – just the right consistency to cover the chicken comfortably. Bake in a moderate oven for ½ hr to 45 minutes or till chicken is done.

Add the butter, milk, seasoning and cheese to the mashed potatoes. (1-2 tblsp mayonnaise could also be added if desired.) Stir till smooth and creamy. Spread this mixture over the baked chicken. Sprinkle a little more cheese on top if desired. Brown under the grill. A green/tomato salad or coleslaw is a good accompaniment.

BAKED CUBED CHICKEN BREASTS

2 cups chicken breasts cooked, deboned, and cut in bit size

1 cup fresh/dried/canned mushrooms sliced

1 bunch spring onions chopped

1 large onion sliced

1 green capsicum de-seeded and sliced

1 tblsp. flour

1 tblsp. butter/oil

½ cup chicken stock

½ cup milk

2 whole eggs or 4 egg whites

1-2 tblsp. parsley chopped fine

Salt and pepper to taste

1-2 tblsp. grated cheese

Method

Mix the cooked chicken with the onion, capsicum, spring onions and mushrooms. If using fresh or dried mushrooms, wash several times under a running tap and then soak in boiling water for at least 15 minutes. Make a white sauce by stirring melted butter/oil and flour over low flame till blended and then gradually add the milk and stock stirring continuously till thick. Remove from heat and add the cheese seasoning. Add sauce to the chicken mixture. Next add the parsley and fold in the eggs mixing well. If using only egg whites, then beat them stiff before folding in to the mixture lightly. Place the mixture in an oven proof dish and bake in a moderate oven till set. Cut in serving pieces or squares and serve with mashed creamed potatoes/ herbed buttered small potatoes and a green salad.

CHICKEN PANCAKES AU GRATIN

(This could be made with any left-over chicken or fresh chicken filling. Below is a suggested recipe for filling. However, any other filling of choice may be used. Chicken may be substituted with fish or any other red meat mince – leftovers or freshly cooked. Whatever the filling this can be an economical and yet a tasty main dish.)

6 oz. plain white flour	A pinch of salt
1 egg or, ½ tsp. baking powder	¾ pint milk (more or less) or, ½ milk & ½ water
Oil for frying	

Pancakes:

Sieve flour, salt and baking powder if using. Add the egg, if using and lightly mix. Next add enough liquid to form a medium thin batter of pouring consistency. The batter should neither be too watery nor too thick. Use a non-stick small fry pan or a small heated, lightly oiled griddle. Spread batter on pan with a rounded spoon spreading it out from the centre to the edge of the pan in a circular motion. Alternately pour batter from a jug and tilt pan in a circular motion to spread evenly. When bubbles form carefully turn pancake with a wooden spatula. Let cook for a few seconds. Take off heat and keep warm. Do not overcook or it will be difficult to roll the pancakes with the filling. The pancakes should be the size of a small saucer. Cook the rest of the pancakes similarly. Makes about 12 to 18 pancakes.

Filling:

4 oz. cooked, de-boned chicken cut up small	1 small or, ¼ green pepper (capsicum) finely cut
2 cups white sauce	

Mix all the above with only 1 cup of white sauce till of a filling consistency. Keep aside the rest of the white sauce.

Method:

Put a teaspoon or a little more filling in the centre of each pancake. fold the two sides gently over the filling. Grease a large oven proof dish well. Lay the pancakes side by side in the dish with the fold side down. Try not to let the pancakes overlap. if necessary, use more than one dish. Rectangular or a square dish is good for this.

Add 2-4 tblsp of grated cheddar cheese to the I cup of white sauce kept in reserve. Mix well. This should be done while the sauce is still hot. At this time also add 1 beaten egg – optional. If necessary, add another ½ or 1 cup of white sauce. Add the cheese and egg accordingly. Pour this sauce over the pancakes till all well covered. Fill the cracks, crevices if any, and the sides well. Dot top with melted butter. Sprinkle parmesan cheese over the top of the dish. Place under a hot grill till well browned. Serve with a green salad or a tomato salad.

Variations:

1. 2-3 tblsp mayonnaise can be added to the final sauce before pouring over the pancakes. This gives it an extra flavour. The eggs could be omitted.
2. 1-2 cans of tuna with mayonnaise make a good filling. Chopped capsicum and chopped spring onions could be mixed with the tuna.
3. Sausage meat or canned luncheon meat could also be used the same way as the tuna.
4. Chopped ham is another variation of a filling which should be mixed with white sauce like the chicken filling.

GRILLED CHICKEN

2 young spring chickens

2 tblsp. onion paste

1 tblsp. Worcestershire sauce

Salt and pepper to taste

2 tsp. ginger paste

2 tsp. garlic paste

2 tblsp. red (preferably wine) vinegar

4 tblsp. oil

Method

Marinate the chickens with all the above ingredients over night or for several hours. Grill on charcoal or an electric or gas grill basting with the marinade from time to time. Turn chickens frequently till done. They should be a golden-brown colour. A rotisserie can also be used to grill the chickens – this way they will have an even colour. The chickens should take about ½ hour to 45 minutes be ready. Serve hot, whole, or halved.

<u>Accompaniments</u>:

8 medium partially boiled potatoes, peeled, rolled in the marinade, and grilled. Baste with the marinade from time to time as with the chickens.

A combination of boiled carrots and green string beans, cut small and mixed with parsley or mint butter.

BAR-B-Q'ED OR GRILLED CHICKEN TENGRI (LEG)

8 chicken legs skin removed	Salt to taste
1 tsp. turmeric powder	3 tblsp. yogurt unsweetened
2 tsp. garlic paste	2 tsp. ginger paste
2 tblsp. onion paste	1 tsp. chilli powder (optional)
2-4 tblsp./ oil	1 tblsp. tomato purée or, 1-2 tsp. red food colouring or, degi/kashmirimirchi" for colouring

Method

Make gashes on the chicken legs. Rub legs with salt and turmeric powder. Combine yogurt, garlic, ginger, onion pastes, chilli powder and oil and marinate chicken legs in this. Leave for several hours preferably overnight in the refrigerator turning from time to time for the marinade to penetrate from all sides. Rub tomato puree or colouring just before barbecuing or grilling. Keep turning the legs to cook evenly applying more oil from time to time. Take off heat when ready. Should be slightly burnt and "reddish". Pierce with a toothpick to make sure the legs are cooked inside. Serve hot with thin slices of raw onions and lime.

YAKITORI – CHICKEN SHEESH KEBAB JAPANESE STYLE

Chicken as much as required

Capsicum as much as required

Skewers (preferably bamboo) as many as required

Spring onions as much as required

½ tsp. ajinomoto, gourmet powder or sugar

Salt to taste

Method

Cut chicken and vegetable in strips or pieces. Cut spring onion and capsicum in small pieces. Sprinkle with ajinomoto or substitute and salt. Arrange skewers with alternate layers of chicken, spring onion and capsicum. Place skewers on a barbecue or any small or medium charcoal burner or alternatively under a grill or broiler. (A barbecue or charcoal burner is best suited for making yakitori). Cook till half done turning the skewers from time to time. Now dip each skewer in the sauce till well soaked and return to burner. The flame of the burner should be even at all times – not too high and not too low. When yakitori is ready, take off heat and once again dip in the sauce before serving. The remaining sauce may then be heated once again and served separately with the yakitori. The whole process should not take more than 10 minutes. Excellent dish to serve with drinks.

Marinade & Sauce:

¼ cup boiling water

2 tsp. white or golden sweet wine (preferably Japanese)

¼ tsp. soup powder or, chicken bouillon cube

4 tblsp. sugar

½ cup soy sauce

Add all the above ingredients to the boiling water and cook for a couple of minutes till the sugar melts. Remove from heat and keep aside.

Note:

If making yakitori under a grill or broiler use wood smoke oil (available abroad but now also available in India in most metropolitan large grocery shops) in the marinade or sprinkled on the skewers to get the smoky taste. 1-2 tsp of oil is all that is required or follow instructions on the bottle.

CRUMB FRIED CHICKEN CUTLETS

250 gm. ground chicken preferably breasts

2 tblsp. coriander leaves finely chopped

1-2 tblsp. ketchup

1 tblsp. Worcestershire or soy sauce

2 eggs

1-2 tblsp. dry flour

1 cup (more or less) breadcrumbs

1-2 tblsp. parsley leaves

1 slice bread soaked in 2-4 tblsp. milk

1 large onion minced

½ tsp. ginger paste (optional)

Salt and pepper to taste

1 tblsp. milk

¼ cup oil for frying

1 fresh green chilli de-seeded and minced (optional)

Method

Mix chicken with the soaked and crumbled bread, onion, coriander leaves, green chilli sauces, paste, 1 egg, salt & pepper. Blend all well, if necessary, in a food processor. Shape into 4 large, flat, slightly oval cutlets. Stick a chicken leg bone in one corner. Dust cutlets in dry flour and let rest for about 5 minutes. Beat 1 egg with the milk and dip cutlets in the mixture carefully, then roll in breadcrumbs covering all sides. Rest for 15-20 minutes. Heat oil in a large shallow fry pan and fry the cutlets carefully on medium to low heat. Turn cutlets over when one side is browned. Stick a skewer or fork in the centre to check the doneness. Dry fry parsley leaves in a non-stick griddle till crisp. Crumble and sprinkle over cutlets. Serve hot with French fries and a green or tomato onion salad.

BLACK PEPPER CHICKEN FRY

1 small chicken jointed in medium size pieces	1 tsp. ginger juice
2 tsp. or more pepper corns freshly ground	1 tsp. garlic juice
2 tblsp. onion juice	2 tblsp. Worcestershire sauce
1 tblsp. vinegar	Salt to taste
¼ tsp. sugar	Oil for frying

Method

Soak chicken in the above ingredients for about 2 hours or more. It can also be soaked overnight. Roll pieces in dry flour and rest for about ½ hour. Shallow fry in oil or butter on very low flame turning constantly so that the pieces get cooked evenly. Alternately make a light batter with 1 egg, milk or water, flour or a paste of just plain flour and cold water or, roll chicken pieces in a paste of flour and cold water or just plain dry flour, and deep fry.

QUICK CHICKEN STIR FRY

500 gm. shredded chicken

2 large potatoes cubed small

3 or 4 tblsp. oil

250 gm. chopped spring onions

1 dry red chilli de-seeded

Salt to taste

Method

Heat oil in fry pan. Add whole dry chilli. Now add all the rest of the ingredients and fry gently till all well-cooked. This dish tastes better when cooked in a little more oil. However, if required the oil content may be reduced. Serve with either plain boiled rice or any type of Indian bread. 1 or 2 tblsp of green peas may also be added. If peas are frozen then add towards the end of cooking.

CHICKEN FRIED IN CHEESE BATTER

2 large chicken legs cut in four (drumsticks and thighs)

½ tsp. baking powder

½ cup oil or less for frying

Sufficient water or milk for the batter

Paprika to taste (optional)

2 tblsp. lime juice or milk

Salt and pepper to taste

1 cup grated any cooking cheese or parmesan

1 cup flour sieved

Method

Soak the chicken pieces in the lime juice or milk for several hours to get rid of the "fowl" smell. Keep aside 1-2 tblsp. flour. Sift the rest of the flour with all the dry ingredients except the cheese. Now add the cheese and make sure it is well blended. Make a thick batter with sufficient water or milk. Rest for ½ -1 hr. Dry chicken pieces with paper towels. Roll in 2 tblsp. dry flour. Rest for 5 minutes. Heat oil. Dip chicken in the cheese batter and fry gently on low-medium heat turning frequently to form an even golden brown. Pierce with a fork or skewer to test the doneness of the chicken. Drain on paper towel. Serve with mashed potato, mashed lemon green papaya (see the vegetable section) and any green or tomato salad.

CHINESE FRIED CHICKEN

Large spring chicken (approx. 1 kg.) cut in serving pieces (approx. 12 pcs.)	2 tblsp. dark soy sauce
1 medium onion minced fine	Salt to taste
¼ cup dry sherry or brandy	2 tblsp. sesame oil
½ tsp. sugar	2 cups oil for frying
1-2 cup dry white flour	

Method

Mix all the above ingredients except flour and oil for frying. Marinate the chicken pieces in it for 1-2 hrs or more. Better still if it is kept in the refrigerator overnight. Take out of marinade and roll in dry flour till chicken pieces are well covered. Deep fry in hot oil till golden brown -- approximately 5-6 minutes. Drain on paper towel before serving. Serve with *lomein* or plain Chinese noodles and the following sauce.

Sauce:

2-3 bunches spring onions chopped fine	3-4 cloves garlic chopped fine
1 tsp. sesame oil	1 cup chicken stock or chicken bouillon cube diluted in 1½ cups hot water
2 tsp. corn flour	1-2 green chillis chopped fine

Fry the spring onions and garlic lightly in the oil. Add to the stock with the chillis and simmer for about 2-3 minutes. Thicken with the corn flour.

CHILLI CHICKEN

500 gm. chicken skinned, de-boned and diced	3 tblsp. flour
1-2 tblsp. light soy sauce	2 tsp. chilli sauce (more or less)
½ tsp. black pepper freshly ground	A large pinch monosodium glutamate (ajinomoto) or sugar
Salt to taste	1-2 tblsp. oil
1 strand spring onion chopped fine	

Method

Roll chicken cubes in flour and let rest for 5-10 minutes. Heat oil and fry chicken cubes till golden brown and cooked. Add all the other ingredients except spring onions and stir fry for a couple of minutes. Place on serving dish and sprinkle with the spring onion.

Variation:

Mince left over chilli chicken and form into patties. Brush non-stick fry pan with oil and cook patties till golden brown. Place in between hamburger buns with sliced cheese and tomatoes and lettuce. All or any of the latter three items can be used in the hamburger according to choice.

Alternately left- over chilli chicken can be used as a filling for *'paratha'* rolls

FRIED CHICKEN A LA MUSLIM

1 spring chicken (500-800gm.)	Salt to taste
1½" pc. ginger ground	8 large cloves garlic ground
1-2 cups of water	1 cup breadcrumbs

Method

Rub inside and outside of chicken with salt. Leave to dry. Next smear ginger and garlic paste well all over the chicken. Place in a deep pan. Add just enough water to cover chicken. Cover with a tightly fitting lid and simmer on low heat till tender. Drain chicken of all liquid and leave a few minutes to dry out. The chicken should not be over cooked. Roll the whole chicken in breadcrumbs till totally covered. Rest a few minutes. Finally cover with the beaten egg. Heat oil in a wok and deep fry chicken gently till a nice golden brown. Drain on paper towel. Serve whole or cut in serving pieces with a simple salad.

<u>Salad options</u>:

1. <u>Cabbage Salad</u>

5-8 cabbage leaves grated fine	1 medium carrot grated fine
1 small capsicum grated	1 small cucumber grated
Salt, pepper, and chilli powder to taste	2 tblsp or to taste fresh lime juice
1 small onion minced (optional)	

Mix the above together. Chill

2. <u>Tomato Salad</u>

3-4 red ripe firm tomatoes	1 medium onion sliced fine
1-2 strands spring onions minced fine	¼ tsp. mustard powder
1 tsp. fine sugar	Salt and pepper to taste
2 tblsp. fresh lime juice or, 1 tblsp. good wine vinegar	

Mix all the above together. Chill.

3. Cucumber Salad

1 large cucumber peeled and grated. Rub with salt and leave for a few minutes. Squeeze out the water. Mix with salt and pepper to taste and fresh lime juice.

CHICKEN MUSLIM STYLE

(This dish is rather rich though not very spicy. A lot of yogurt, onions, ginger, and garlic are used. This is normally cooked in a lot of ghee (clarified butter) to give it a rich texture. However, oil is suggested in the recipe below. The ingredients have also been cut down from the original recipe. If preferred the measurements can be increased or decreased according to taste, as the recipe is very flexible.)

1½-2 kg. chicken cut in serving pieces	3-4 cups of yogurt
3-4 cups of oil	8-10 tblsp. or more ground onion
1-2 tblsp. ground ginger	1-2 tblsp. ground garlic
1 tsp. or more turmeric, if a little colour is desired	Salt to taste

Method

Marinate the chicken pieces in the yogurt for a couple of hours or more. Warm oil and fry well the onion, ginger, garlic, and turmeric if used. Add the chicken pieces minus the marinade. Continue frying till a nice golden brown and coated with the spices. Now add the yogurt marinade and continue cooking till the chicken is done and most of the yogurt has been absorbed. The gravy should be fairly thick. Serve with any Indian bread and an Indian salad.

Variation:

Mughlai Chicken:

Marinate the chicken as above. Before frying the ground spices put the following in the heated oil. 2-3 bay leaves, 4-6 cardamoms, 6-8 cloves and 2" piece cinnamon. When they start to splutter add the ground spices and continue as above.

When the chicken is done and most of the curd has been absorbed add 1-2 tblsp rose water for flavouring. At this point also add 8-10 whole raisins washed and 4-6 almonds cut in slivers.

Fry 2-3 large onion slices brown and sprinkle over chicken as garnish before serving.

CHOPPED CHICKEN LIVER

500 gm. chicken liver chopped coarsely

6 eggs boiled

500 gm. onion chopped

½ cup olive oil + ½ tblsp. white/olive oil

Salt and pepper to taste

Method

Smear chicken livers with a little oil and grill or cook on top of the stove till done. Fry the onions in the extra oil till transparent. Now put the liver, onions, and eggs in the food processor till smooth and well mixed. Add the rest of the olive oil and seasoning and stir to mix. Serve hot or cold on toasts or crackers which can be served as hors d'oeuvres or with drinks. Alternately pack in a round mould and then turn out on to a flat dish lined with lettuce. Garnish top with 3-4 fresh basil/mint leaves. Surround base with a few slices of cucumber and tomatoes. This can be served as a first course at a buffet dinner or lunch.

Variation:

Chicken liver can be substituted with either, beef, pork or lamb which should be sliced before grilling. If the liver has too much fat, then reduce the oil content.

CREAMED CHICKEN AND NOODLE

1-1½ kg. chicken
1 large onion
4-6 whole black peppercorns
1 cup water
2 tblsp. sherry
¾ cup button mushrooms

1 large carrot
3-4 tblsp. celery leaves
Salt to taste
2 cups thick white sauce
1 cup fresh cream
350 gm. (or more) egg noodles

Method

Cook chicken with carrot, onion, celery leaves, peppercorns, and salt in 1 cup of water. When done cut chicken up in small pieces preferably de-boned. Mash the vegetables in the stock. Make the white sauce. Cool. Add the sherry, cream, mashed vegetables with the stock, chicken pieces and the mushrooms. Cook the noodles and gently toss into the chicken mixture. Serve hot garnished with parsley sprigs.

<u>*White Sauce*</u>:

In a saucepan mix 2-3 tblsp butter/margarine, 1 med onion chopped, 2-3 tblsp heaped flour. Cook on low heat stirring continuously with a wooden ladle till well mixed and the onion becomes transparent. Add 1 pt. milk gradually, stirring all the time. Cook till thick making sure no lumps form.

NOKY (NOODLES) WITH CHICKEN SAUCE – CZECH STYLE

Noky:

1-2 eggs	1 cup water
Salt to taste	500 gm. flour
1 tblsp. oil	

Sauce for Noky:

2 large onions chopped	2 tblsp. oil
1 large chicken skin removed, cleaned, and jointed	2 cups water
1 tblsp. tomato purée	1 tsp. sweet paprika
1 tsp. hot paprika	¼ litre cream
2 tblsp. flour or, corn flour	Salt to taste

Method

Noky:

Combine eggs and water and beat well with an electric hand beater or in the blender. Add the rest of the ingredients and mix well into a stiff dough. Knead the dough well in a food processor or with the back of the hand. Cover with a tea towel or cheese cloth and let it rest for 1 hour. Now take the dough a little at a time and cut into small strips. Bring water and salt to the boil and drop the noky into it. Cook for 10-15 mins or take one out and test for doneness. When ready rinse in a colander under a cold-water tap. Toss the noky with a little oil so that they do not stick and get soggy. The noky can be reheated and served with any sauce of one's choice. Given below is a chicken sauce.

Sauce for Noky:

Sauté the onions lightly in the oil. Add the chicken pieces and fry lightly with the salt till white in color. Add the water, tomato purée and the sweet and hot paprika and cook till chicken is done. Alternately pressure cook for 20 minutes. When done take the chicken out and add the cream and flour to the sauce and keep stirring over low heat or in a double boiler for a few seconds or until the sauce begins to thicken. Place the chicken back in the sauce and serve with the noky.

KOWSHWE

(This is a great dish for informal large gatherings or even to serve up to the family. This is best eaten in large individual bowls or soup plates with spoon and fork as there is a lot of liquid involved. Well-made it is always a success.)

1.5-2 kg. chicken cut in medium pieces	Salt and pepper to taste
1 tsp. heaped turmeric powder	2 litre water or more
3-4 tsp. ginger paste	4 fresh green chillis ground (optional)
2 tsp. garlic paste	1 cup onion paste
4 tblsp. oil	1 large onion sliced
1 tblsp besan (chickpea flour) dry roasted	3-4 cups thick coconut milk
2 kg. spaghetti or egg noodles, (not too fine) cooked *al denté*	

Accompaniments:

1 cup vermicelli cut and dry roasted brown	2-3 limes cut in eighths
1-2 medium cucumber grated	4-5 medium tomatoes chopped
1 thick bunch spring onions chopped	1-2 green peppers de-seeded and chopped
2-3 fresh green chillis de-seeded and chopped (optional)	1 bulb garlic peeled, cut small, roasted dry or fried in a little oil
3 hard-boiled eggs cut-up small	1 bunch coriander leaves chopped
2 medium onions minced	

Method

Rub cut chicken with salt and a little turmeric powder. Cook in saucepan with water till tender. Cool. De-bone the chicken pieces getting as much meat out as possible. Alternatively, de-bone chicken before cooking. Cut into small pieces and cook with the bones. If some of the chicken pieces are a little too large cut them up into small pieces. Put the bones back into the chicken stock and cook some more. Take the bones out and cool. Crack them and take the marrow out. Put this into the stock and throw all the bones away. Let stock simmer on very low heat for about 10-15 minutes. In the meantime, rub the cooked chicken pieces with all the pastes and any left-over turmeric. Heat oil. Fry onions brown. Add the chicken and fry some more. Add the stock and keep on simmer. Make a paste of the 'besan' in some water. Stir it into the chicken and simmer for another 10 minutes. Keep stirring during this time. Add the coconut milk and simmer for 10-15 minutes. Take off heat and serve with the spaghetti separately or together with the chicken poured over it.

Put all the accompaniments in separate bowls and serve with the kowshwe. These are sprinkled over the kowshwe with a squeeze of lemon by the individual diner according to taste.

FRIED DUCK WITH THICK SPICY GRAVY

1 large duck jointed	1 large bulb garlic crushed or pounded
2" or 3" piece ginger crushed and pounded	2 tblsp' sherry or, red wine or, brandy or, 1 tblsp. red wine & 1 tblsp. brandy
1 tsp. freshly ground black pepper	3 tblsp. soy sauce
2 tsp. sesame oil	Water

Method

Soak duck pieces in a combination of the above marinade excluding the sesame oil, overnight. In a large pan fry duck in very hot oil. Add enough warm water to cover duck. Cover pan. Cook in a slow oven till duck pieces are tender. Alternately the pieces may be cooked on top of the stove covered on low heat till done. Scrape the pan juices and pour over the duck before serving. If too dry add a little warm water to the pan juices and bring to boil. Simmer for a couple of minutes and pour over the duck.

Variations:

Chicken may be cooked as above. Large chunks of pork, beef or mutton may also be cooked in a similar way. The quantity of spices and salt may be adjusted according to taste. Just before serving split deseeded green chillis may be used as garnish. If preferred, 1 split de-seeded red chilli maybe fried with the duck or meat pieces. This dish may also be made with a whole duck or chicken or a joint of any of the red meats. In that case it will need extra slow cooking and constant turning to make sure of even cooking. Though this may sound a little tedious and time consuming, the ultimate result will bring many kudos to the hostess!

MUMMY'S DUCK HAARI ('COOKING POT') KABAB

My mother was famous for her Haari Kabab, but she never had a fixed proportion of ingredients and made it every time based on her instincts. I have tried to give representative amounts, but please feel free to experiment according to taste.

1 large, young, fat duck

Marinade:

2" or 3" piece ginger crushed and pounded	1 tsp. garam masala (equal mixture of powdered cinnamon, cloves, and cardamom) made into a paste with a little bit of water
2-4 onions freshly ground	1 large bulb garlic crushed or pounded
2-4 bay leaves	1 cup yogurt
1 tsp. coriander powder or more depending on the size of the duck	1 tsp. cumin powder or more depending on the size of the duck
2 tblsp. ground raisins (raisins should be ground into a paste and not whole)	½ cup red wine

Method

Select a young, big fat duck. After washing and cleaning thoroughly, dry with a kitchen towel. Leave for 15 mins. Rub the duck thoroughly inside and outside with the following marinade:

Marinade:

Use plenty of ground onion, ginger, garlic. Add the bay leaves and a small amount of garam masala powder comprising equal amount of, cloves, cinnamon, and cardamom, powders. Also add the coriander and cumin powders. Make all these powders into a paste with a little water. Add yogurt and plenty of ground raisins. Red wine may also be added.

Duck:

Fry whole duck gently on top of the stove in oil till golden brown. Cook in a pressure cooker with sufficient water. When ready it should have a very little thick gravy. Alternately cook in a moderately hot oven. I get the best results when baked using a clay pot, such as a Römertopf in the oven (Römertopf is a European clay pot with a lid).

LAMB & MUTTON

LAMB CHOPS

1 large or 2 medium lamb chops per person

½ tsp. garlic paste

1 tsp. wine vinegar

1 medium onion sliced

¼ tsp. bouillon cube powdered (optional)

1 cup water (approximate)

½ tsp. ginger paste

1 tsp. Worcestershire sauce

1 tblsp. oil

1 medium potato sliced

Salt and pepper to taste

Method

Marinate chops in ginger, garlic paste, Worcestershire sauce, wine vinegar for 1 hour or more. On low flame heat oil in a heavy bottomed pan. Lay chops, onions, and potatoes evenly and let cook on both sides till all change colour. The chops should be seared while the onions and potatoes should become transparent. (The chops maybe seared on both sides first and then the onions and potatoes added. They should be cooked till transparent. If required, the chops may be put aside till the onions and potatoes are cooked. Return the chops to the pan and continue.) Add all the other ingredients including the marinade. Let cook for 5 minutes. Add enough water to cover chops. Cover and cook till soft.

Serve with a mixture of boiled rice, peas and cubes of carrots tossed in 1 tsp. butter or olive oil. Sprinkle with chopped mint and toss. This may be served hot or in room temperature.

BREADED LAMB CHOPS

1 large or 2 medium chops per person

1 tsp. Worcestershire or light soy sauce

Salt & pepper to taste

1 egg

Oil for frying

1 tsp. vinegar

½ tsp. each of onion, ginger & garlic paste

1 tblsp. sifted flour

4 tblsp. fine breadcrumbs

Method

Mix all above ingredients except egg, flour, breadcrumbs, and oil. Marinate chops in this mixture for 1 hr. or more. Spread the flour on a plate or kitchen paper. Roll chops in it and keep aside for about 10-15 minutes. Beat eggs. Spread breadcrumbs on a flat tray, plate, or kitchen paper. Dip chops in the egg and roll in breadcrumbs. Repeat once more. Make sure the chops are coated well all around. Keep aside for half an hour or more. Heat oil on low flame in a heavy bottomed shallow pan. Fry chops slowly on both sides making sure they do not get burnt. Drain on paper towel and serve immediately. Do not overheat oil or else the chops will brown quickly on the outside and remain uncooked inside. They should be a golden colour on the outside and tender inside.

Serve with a tomato sauce, creamed potato and either a green salad or tomato salad.

Tomato Sauce:

In a bowl mix 2 tblsp. ketchup or tomato paste, ¼ tsp. ginger powder, ¼ tsp. garlic powder, 1 tsp. honey. paprika and salt to taste. Add 1 tblsp. of water if necessary.

Creamed Potato:

Steam and mash potato till fluffy. Add salt, pepper to taste. For 1 large potato add 1-2tblsp. milk, 1 tblsp. butter. Mix all well. Mould in a greased bowl. Turn over onto a flat dish before serving. Make etchings with a fork on the sides and top.

LAMB CHOPS CASSEROLE

1-2 tblsp. of oil or more	1 large or 2 medium chops per person
1 large potato sliced thickly	1 large carrot sliced lengthwise
1 bay leaf	3-4 cloves
1 small cinnamon	2-3 green cardamoms
2 tsp. Worcestershire sauce	4-6 whole black peppercorns
Salt to taste	1 cup hot water or more
4 tblsp. tomato purée	1 large onion sliced thickly
¼ bouillon cube powdered	4-6 thin slices of ginger

Method

Heat oil in a heavy bottomed pan. Sear chops on both sides put in an ovenproof casserole with cover. Next brown potatoes and carrots and put on top of chops. Now put bay leaf, cloves, cinnamon, cardamom, and peppercorns in the pan with the oil. When they start spluttering add the sauce, seasoning, puree, bouillon cube, onion, and ginger slices. Mix all and add the hot water. When it comes to boil pour it over the chops in the casserole. Cover and cook in a medium pre-heated oven till done. More than one cup of water may be needed. The water should come 1" above the chops and vegetables.

Variations:

3-4 tblsp. left over rice could also be added after the vegetables. If using uncooked rice then this should be put with the onions and ginger. This is a complete meal dish and is easy to prepare for the bachelor or busy housewife or working girl. It is nourishing too!

LAMB CASSEROLE

1 kg. shoulder of lamb, fat trimmed and cubed	1 tblsp. lemon rind thinly sliced
1-2 bay leaves	½" ginger finely minced
2 large onions chopped roughly	1 tsp. paprika
½ tsp. mixed spice (optional)	Salt and freshly ground pepper to taste
2 tblsp. heaped flour	2 tblsp. butter or oil
4 tblsp. cream	2 tblsp. heaped milk powder
1½ pt. cold water (approx.)	

Method

Put meat pieces in a saucepan covering with cold water. Bring to boil and let boil for 15 minutes to ½ hour or till meat is half cooked. Remove all the scum with a spoon. Strain the liquid. (Alternately, pressure cook for 15-20 minutes. Turn off heat, cool, open lid and remove all the scum. Strain the liquid.) Place the meat and the liquid in an ovenproof dish. Add all the ingredients except butter/oil, flour, and cream. Cook in a slow oven till meat is done. Melt the butter in a saucepan, add the flour and stir for a few minutes till well blended. Do not let it burn. Gradually add 3 cups of the liquid from the lamb stirring continuously. Cook till sauce begins to thicken. Add all the meat mixture and the milk powder to the sauce and cook another few minutes till all well blended. Let it cool slightly. Stir in the cream and serve.

Variation:

Add 1 or 2 carrots sliced, 2 potatoes sliced thickly, and a handful of peas with the meat in the casserole before placing the dish into the oven. This way it will need no other accompaniment and becomes a dish in itself. ¼ cup cooked rice can also be thrown in with the meat. Alternatively, add cooked macaroni.

STEWED LAMB CHOPS

4 lean lamb chops	1 tblsp. oil
2-3 medium potatoes sliced	1-2 large carrots cut into 3-4 pieces
1 large onion thickly sliced	1-2 tblsp. Worcestershire or any other sauce
2-3 spring onions cut in 1" strips	1-2 red pepper de-seeded and sliced
1 small celery stem thickly sliced	1 tsp fresh or dried rosemary leaves
1-2 cups of water	

Method

Trim the fat from the lamb chops if necessary. Put the oil in a large and wide nonstick pan. Brown the potatoes and carrots evenly. Put aside till required. Now brown the chops and the onion in the same pan with the Worcester sauce. Next add the browned vegetables, spring onions, red pepper, celery, rosemary, and the water. When the stew comes to a boil lower the heat, cover the pan, and cook till meat and vegetables are done. There should be a thick gravy. Serve with a border of rice / pasta or pita bread or dumplings.

Variations:

After the above comes to a boil transfer to an oven proof/microwave safe dish and either cook covered in a medium hot oven or microwave. If dumplings are being served as accompaniment they can be dropped into the pan with the chops and vegetables.

KASHMIRI MUTTON CHOPS

8 lean mutton chops	5-6 whole green/black pepper corns
1 tblsp. onion paste	4-5 green cardamoms or, 1 large cardamom split
1 tsp. ginger paste	¼ - ½ tsp. garlic paste
1" piece cinnamon stick	1 tsp. whole cumin
¼ tsp. whole fennel/anise	1-2 bay leaves
½ litre (more or less) fresh creamy milk	1-2 tsp. saffron soaked in 1 tblsp. warm milk
1 tsp 'degi mirch' or Kashmiri chilli powder	Salt and pepper to taste
2-4 tblsp. oil	

Method

Cook all the above ingredients together till mutton is soft and the milk has thickened to almost being dry as in "*khoa*". Next fry the chops along with all the spices and the dried milk till well browned. Discard all the whole spices before serving. Serve with any Indian bread .and salad. Garnish chops with either fresh coriander, or mint or basil leaves.

SATÉ KAMBING – INDONESIAN SHEESH KEBAB

1 kg. lamb cut in serving pieces

1 tsp. garlic paste

1 tsp. black pepper

3 tblsp. oil

500 gm. lamb fat cut in small cubes (optional)

1 tblsp. onion paste

1 tsp. nutmeg

1 tblsp. sugar

4 tblsp. soy sauce

Method

Marinate the lamb cubes in a mixture of onion and garlic paste, ground nutmeg and black pepper, sugar and 1 tblsp oil overnight. The next day, mix the rest of the oil with the soy sauce and keep aside. Skewer the lamb in Shish kebab skewers (bamboo skewers are preferable), alternating with pieces of fat which makes the saté tender and moist. Dip the skewers generously in the oil/soy mixture and barbecue or put under the grill or on top of the gas ring. Serve with the following peanut sauce.

Peanut Sauce:

1 tblsp. oil

4 tblsp. ground peanut

1-2 tsp. paprika

4 tblsp. water

1-2 tsp. lemon juice

2 tblsp. onion paste

1 tsp. sugar

Salt to taste

1 tsp. soy sauce

Heat oil and fry the onion paste till light brown. Add all the other ingredients and let it come to boil. Lower heat and simmer till thick. Take off heat. Stir in soy sauce and lemon juice.

ARMENIAN SHEESH KEBAB

1 kg. ground meat (lamb)

¼-½ cup olive oil

1 fresh green chilli de-seeded and chopped

3-4 garlic cloves chopped or, 1 tsp. garlic powder (optional)

½ tsp. cinnamon powder

½ tsp. nutmeg powder

Salt and pepper to taste

Method

Mix and put all the above ingredients in the food processor or through the meat grinder 2 or 3 times. The meat should be ground fine. (The oil in the mixture makes the kebab mixture moist.) Now wet the hands and take the mixture (the size of a finger) a little at a time and stick on a skewer. The mixture should go round the skewer. Brush kebabs with oil if necessary. Grill carefully on charcoal, gas or electric grill turning the skewer round gently to cook all sides. When done carefully slide the kebabs off the skewer. Serve garnished with chopped parsley, raw onions, lemon wedges and thinly sliced cucumber. Baking powder parathas (see under "Bread" in this book series) are a good accompaniment with these shish kebabs.

Variations:

1. Veal may also be used for this kebab. Both lamb and veal are equally good. Ground chicken can also be substituted

2. 1 or 2 chopped onions could be added to the mixture. In this case omit the nutmeg.

3. 1 or 2 tblsp. barbecue sauce or any other sauce of one's choice can be added to the mixture. The sauce added at the last minute just before shaping, add to the taste.

SHAMI KEBAB (I)

1 kg. ground meat	250 gm. nutrela (soy chunks or granules) after soaking in water
1-2 onions minced	1" pc. ginger chopped
3-4 cloves garlic	3-4 cloves
1" pc. cinnamon	salt to taste
2-3 green cardamoms	½ tsp. paprika
1 tsp. each coriander and cumin dry roasted	4 tblsp. gram flour (besan)
1-2 fresh green chillis de-seeded and chopped fine	½ cup (approx.) oil

Method

Pressure cook for 15 minutes or boil all the ingredients together except gram flour, green chillis and oil. Cool and put in a food processor or through a mincer. The mixture should be smooth. Dry roast the gram flour in a griddle to get the raw smell out. Combine with the meat mixture along with the chillis. Form into round kebabs, roll in dry flour and let rest for 10 mins. Fry in batches in a non-stick fry pan or a griddle using very little oil – just enough to brush the pan and drizzle a little on the sides if necessary. The kebabs should be a nice dark brown. Serve garnished with raw onion rings and slices of lime.

Variation:

These kebabs can also be made with ground beef.

SHAMI KEBAB (II)

500 gm. ground meat

1" piece ginger sliced

1-2 bay leaves

5-6 cloves

6-8 whole pepper corns

salt to taste

½ cup (more or less) flour

¼ cup oil (more or less) for frying

2 onions chopped

5-6 cloves garlic (optional)

1" stick cinnamon

3-4 green cardamoms

2 tblsp. gram flour (besan) dry roasted

½ tsp. paprika or one green chilli (optional)

1 small bunch fresh coriander leaves minced fine

Method

Cook the meat with the onions, ginger, garlic, bay leaves, cinnamon, cloves, cardamom, and peppercorns. When cool, grind all very fine in a meat grinder or in a food processor till paste like consistency. Add the gram flour, salt and paprika or green chillis. Mix all well together. Shape into kebabs. Make a depression in the centre of each kebab, fill with minced coriander leaves and cover with the meat from the sides. Flatten slightly, roll in dry flour, and let rest for 5-10 minutes. Shallow fry in a non-stick pan or griddle. Garnish with round slices of cucumber, raw onions, lime and green chillis (optional). Serve as a snack or with any Indian bread.

Note. Besides lamb or mutton *shami* kebabs may also be made with beef. If served as a snack, make the kebab slightly smaller in shape.

HAMBURGER CUTLETS

500 gm. meat ground

1 large onion minced fine

Salt and pepper to taste

2 tblsp. ketchup or, tomato purée

1-2 eggs

1 small green chilli de-seeded and chopped fine

2 slices of stale bread

$1/4$ - $1/2$ garam masala powder

1 tblsp. Worcestershire sauce

1 tblsp. fresh coriander/mint leaves chopped fine

2-4 tblsp. dry flour for dusting

2-4 tblsp. oil for frying

Method

Mix all the above ingredients except the flour and oil together and put in the blender or food processor. Shape into round burghers roll in dry flour and shallow fry over medium heat till nicely browned and the inside when pricked with a toothpick comes out clean. Serve with any green salad. These cutlets can also be placed in between bread rolls with lettuce, tomato, cheese, fried egg etc. and served as hamburgers with a favourite sauce. It can also be served with a tomato or brown sauce/gravy.

Note. The hamburgers can also be made with beef

CHEESE & PINEAPPLE HAMBURGER

1-2 onions minced	1 tblsp flour
1-2 tblsp. oil	1-2 tblsp. pineapple syrup/juice
1-2 tblsp. celery leaves minced	1-2 bouillon cubes crumbled
1-2 tblsp. ketchup/tomato purée /Worcestershire sauce	¼ cup any red wine
1-2 tsp. dried mixed herbs	1-2 tblsp. honey
Salt and pepper to taste	½ tsp. paprika (optional)
Pineapple slices as required	Cheese slices as required
½-¾ cup water	

Method

Slightly brown onion and flour mixed together in oil. Add all the other ingredients except pineapple and cheese slices and bring to the boil. Lower heat and place the burgers in it carefully. Cook till burgers are slightly soft and the gravy thickens. In this recipe, the burgers are not shaped into rounds. Place a slice of pineapple on top of each burger inside the bun followed by a slice of cheese. Continue cooking till cheese melts. Alternately place under the grill just before serving. Served with creamed, mashed potatoes and a salad.

BATTERED MEAT

500 gm. ground meat/mince

2 large onions minced finely

1 green pepper minced finely

1 bunch fresh coriander leaves chopped fine

1 tsp. paprika (optional)

½-1 cup oil for deep frying

Salt and pepper to taste

Batter:

8-10 oz. flour

2 tblsp. heaped baking powder

½ cup water/milk or ½ water and ½ milk

Method

Sift flour and baking powder together. Add enough water, milk or half water and half milk to form a smooth batter – not too thick and not too thin. Keep aside for ½ hour. Mix the ground meat with the rest of the ingredients and form into small balls the size of golf balls. Dip the balls into the batter with a spoon or hand, to coat well. Deep fry. These balls may also be shallow fried in a non-stick fry pan, in which case the oil required will be less. In the latter case the battered mince will not remain round but will spread and will be more on the flat side. If shallow frying, coat the balls with the batter more thickly. In either case they should be crisp and golden. Serve hot with any sauce, pickle, or chutney. The battered meat can be served with drinks or tea/coffee or even as a main course for lunch/dinner accompanied with mashed potatoes and a salad. If serving as a main course, the battered meat should be a little larger.

Note. Beef, pork, chicken or fish can be used instead of lamb. In using fish, steam and de bone before mixing with the other ingredients.

YOUVOURLAKIA OR UNDRESSED DOLMAS

(This is basically a Greek dish and should take about ½ hour cooking time.)

1 tblsp. parsley chopped	1 tblsp. mint leaves chopped
1 tblsp. dill leaves chopped	1 kg. ground meat
1 tblsp. onion grated	2 tblsp. uncooked rice
3 whites of eggs	Salt and pepper to taste
1 tblsp. olive oil	Flour for coating
1 pt. stock or, water	1 tblsp. butter

Method

Mix the parsley, mint, and dill with 1 tblsp of water to hold the herbs together. Now combine this with all the above ingredients except the water and butter. Make into small balls like "koftas". Roll the meat balls in flour to coat. Bring the stock/water with the butter to boiling. Drop the meat balls gently into the boiling liquid and cook till done – approximately ½ hr or when the rice in the meat ball mixture is cooked. Take the balls out of the liquid carefully with a slotted spoon. Reserve the liquid for the sauce. Serve with the following sauce poured over.

Sauce:

1 tblsp. butter	5 tsp. flour
1 tblsp. lemon juice	3 egg yolks beaten
2 tsp. parsley coarsely chopped	

Melt the butter in a saucepan. Add the flour to make a roux. Add the liquid from the meat balls and keep stirring till sauce thickens. Add the lemon juice, stir and take off heat. Add a little bit of the sauce to the egg and stir to mix so that it does not curdle. Add the yolks to the sauce gradually and return to heat for a couple of minutes stirring continuously. Remove from heat and pour over the meat balls. Sprinkle top with chopped parsley.

Variations:

1. Instead of making meat balls the meat mixture can be wrapped in vine leaves. Pour a little hot water over the vine leaves to make them a little

soft and easy to wrap. Arrange the '*dolmas*' in a saucepan. Cover with cold stock or water. Put a lump of butter on top. Press down with a plate and cook on low heat. Take out when ready. Arrange on a flat dish and pour sauce evenly on top. Garnish with chopped parsley.

2. In the absence of vine leaves use tender cabbage leaves. Red pumpkin leaves or spinach leaves can also be substituted. In place of stock/water bouillon cube(s) dissolved in water can also be used.

CLOSED LAHMEDJUN (ARMENIAN)

1 kg. ground meat	3-4 tblsp. onion chopped fine
Salt and freshly ground black pepper to taste	3 tblsp. (more or less) margarine/butter/oil
2 large tomatoes chopped fine	1-2 fresh garlic paste/grated fine
½ tsp. cinnamon powder	¼ tsp. clove powder
Chilli powder to taste	½ tsp. mixed spice powder
1 tblsp. green pepper minus seed chopped fine	1-2 tblsp. fresh/dry mint leaves chopped fine
1-2 tblsp. fresh/dry parsley chopped fine	800 gm. bread or pizza dough

Method

Cook the meat with the onions, salt, and pepper in a little cooking medium for a few mins. When the meat turns brown take off heat and immediately add the tomatoes and stir to mix. Next add all the rest of the ingredients except the dough and cooking medium and again stir well to mix. Refrigerate to cool down.

Take off bits of dough and roll into several large thin "chapatis" or the size required. Place a little meat mixture on one half (the half away from the body) of the "chapati". Fold over with the other half to resemble a half-moon. Press sides down to seal and shape the edges with a pastry cutter. Cut off the extra dough from the edge and keep aside. Prick tops of puffs with a fork to let in air. Do not put too much filling inside the puffs. They should be flat. Shallow fry the puffs by brushing a heavy bottomed or non- stick frying pan with the cooking medium used. The puffs should be fried lightly browned on both sides. Brush pan with melted margarine/butter or oil from time to time as and when necessary. Use up the extra dough cut from the edges in a similar way.

These puffs have a better result when cooked on a heavy iron griddle on charcoal fire. When using an electric or gas cooker, a non-stick pan gives the best result.

MOUSSAKA

12 oz. lamb cooked (grilled/roasted)	1 medium onion chopped
¼ oz. butter/olive oil	3-4 tblsp. ketchup/tomato paste or, purée
1-2 cloves fat garlic crushed	A pinch of grated nutmeg or, ground mace
1 large aubergine sliced	8 oz. tomatoes peeled and sliced
3-4 tblsp. olive oil	2-3 medium potatoes boiled, skinned, peeled
salt and pepper to taste	

Bechamel Sauce:

1 slice onion	2-3 pepper corns
2-3 parsley stalks	7½ liquid oz. milk
¾ oz. butter	1 tblsp. flour
¼ tsp. mustard	Salt to taste
1 egg separated	¼ oz. cheese grated

Method

Dice the meat uniformly. Soften onion in butter till transparent. Add the meat followed by the ketchup/puree. Stir to coat. Add seasoning, garlic, nutmeg, or mace and stir to mix with a wooden spoon. Take off heat and keep aside.

Sprinkle aubergine slices with salt. Drain any water that might come out. Wipe dry with kitchen towel. Shallow fry the slices slightly golden on both sides. Drain on paper towels and keep aside till required.

Now prepare the bechamel sauce. Place the onion, peppercorns, and parsley stalks in a bit of muslin or cheese cloth, tying the ends securely to resemble a pouch. Infuse this into the milk and boil. Take off heat and strain milk. Make a roux of butter and flour and place over low heat. Add the strained milk gradually, stirring continuously so that there are no lumps. When the sauce begins to thicken take off heat and add the mustard and salt to taste. Next beat in the egg yolk. Beat egg white stiff and fold into the sauce. Last of all add the cheese and stir gently. The sauce should not curdle or be lumpy. It should be smooth.

To assemble the moussaka, arrange the meat mixture, potatoes, aubergines, and tomatoes alternately in an oven proof dish. Spoon bechamel sauce over all on top. Bake in a hot oven for about 15-20 minutes or till top is golden and crusty. Serve with any salad of choice.

CREPÉ A LA ROGNON

Pancake Batter:

4 oz. flour	1 tsp. salt
1-2 eggs	¼ cup milk

Filling:

2 tsp. oil	8-10 kidneys chopped fine
1 large capsicum chopped fine	1 large onion chopped fine
2-3 bunches spring onions chopped fine	Salt and pepper to taste
2 tsp. Worcestershire sauce	2 tsp. ketchup (optional)

Method

Make the pancake by sifting the flour and salt. Add the egg slightly beaten one at a time. Next add sufficient milk to form a creamy batter – not too thin and not too thick. It should be spreadable. Keep in a cool place for a couple of hours.

For the filling, warm oil and add all the above ingredients except the sauces and seasonings. Cook till done about 8-10 minutes. Just before removing from heat add the seasonings, Worcestershire sauce and ketchup if using.

Warm a griddle or non-stick heavy bottomed fry pan and put 1 tsp oil, melted butter or margarine. Tilt the pan to cover the surface with the oil. Very quickly pour and spread 1 soup spoon of batter in a circular motion the size of a coffee cup saucer. When bubbles appear place a heaped teaspoon full of filling in the centre of the pancake. Fold in three like an omelette pressing down with the back of the spatula. Take off heat and place in a warm dish till all the pancakes are done. A good supper snack or a first course at dinner.

STEAMED LIVER THE CHINESE WAY

500 gm liver cut in thin strips or slices

1-2 tblsp. light soy sauce

1 pinch of ajinomoto or, brown sugar

1 tsp. fresh ginger finely minced or ground

½ tsp. garlic powder

1 bouillon cube

1 bunch spring onion cut on the slant in strips

1 medium capsicum de-seeded and cut in strips

Method

Add all the above ingredients together and then steam for about 5-10 minutes or till liver is done. Serve with plain steamed rice or fried rice with a cabbage or cucumber salad done the Chinese way – cut in chunks and marinated in a mixture of vinegar or fresh lime juice, chilli powder and salt.

BEEF

GROUND BEEF & BAKED BEANS

1 tblsp. olive oil	2 large onions chopped
2-3 crushed garlic thickly sliced	500 gm. ground beef
1 tblsp. tomato purée	250 gm. baked beans
250 gm. red tomatoes peeled and chopped	½ pt. (10 liquid ounces) water
1 bouillon cube (preferably beef)	2 tsp. Worcestershire or any other dark sauce
1 tblsp. corn starch/corn flour	¼ tsp. paprika (optional)
Salt and pepper to taste	1-2 whole, de-seeded or, chopped green chilli (optional)

Method

Heat oil and lightly brown onions. Add garlic. As garlic begins to brown add ground beef. Cook till colour changes. Add tomato puree and cook another 2 minutes. Transfer meat to casserole. Add baked beans, tomatoes and lightly toss with the meat. In a saucepan bring to boil water and crumbled bouillon cube till the bouillon cube dissolves. Add sauce, stir. Mix corn starch in 1 tblsp. cold water and add to soup stirring constantly till it thickens slightly. Pour over meat and tomatoes. Check for salt and pepper. Paprika maybe added if so desired. Green chillis minus the seeds may also be added if using and gently mixed into the casserole at the end. Bake in moderate oven for 45-50 minutes.

BEEF'N BEANS

1 lb. ground beef	8 oz. can bake beans in tomato sauce
1 tblsp. oil	1 bay leaf
2 medium onions roughly chopped	2-3 cloves garlic crushed
½ tsp. paprika or, according to taste	2 tsp. curry powder
1 tblsp. white flour	3-4 large tomatoes peeled and chopped roughly
10 oz. (more or less) water	1 beef bouillon cube crumbled
Salt and pepper to taste	2 tsp. Worcestershire sauce

Method

Heat oil in a large deep fry pan and add bay leaf. Stir for 1min and then add the onions. When the onions begin to brown add the garlic and brown slightly. Add the beef, stir for a few minutes till meat changes colour. Sprinkle curry powder and paprika on top, stir to mix well and continue to cook till a light brown. Just before taking off the heat add the tomatoes and baked beans. Stir all together and let cook for a couple more minutes. Remove to an oven-proof casserole. In the same fry pan put the flour and bouillon cube. Keep stirring till well mixed. Add the water. Blend well with a wooden spoon till no lumps exist. Bring to the boil. Add the sauces and seasoning, stir, and pour on top of the beef mixture in the casserole. Cover and cook in a moderate oven for about 1 hour. or till done. It should be thickish but not mushy or dry when done. Serve with any salad favoured.

VEAL LOAF

1 kg. veal (beef or lamb may be used) mince.	3 medium onions minced
1 medium capsicum de-seeded and minced.	1 tblsp. parsley chopped
4-5 cloves garlic minced	3 eggs
2 tblsp. breadcrumbs	3 tblsp. oil
6 eggs hard boiled and shelled	4 carrots peeled and boiled

Method

Mix all the minced and chopped ingredients together. Add the eggs and breadcrumbs and mix all well. Fry the mixture lightly in oil. Grease a loaf pan. Line the bottom and sides of the pan with grease proof paper and oil it lightly. Put half the mixture in the base of the pan. Lay the whole eggs in the centre of the mixture. Place the whole carrots on either side of the eggs. Cover with the rest of the meat mixture and press down on top and sides to make the loaf well packed and smooth. Bake in a moderate oven for about 1 hour or till the loaf is done and will not disintegrate when turned out of the tin. Cool on a wire tray and then take out of pan. Cut in slices and serve cold with slices of tomato, cucumber, beetroot etc. on a bed of lettuce. Alternately serve warm with a brown sauce.

Brown Sauce:

Brown 1 heaped tblsp flour in a saucepan. Add 2 cups water gradually and keep stirring reducing the heat till sauce thickens. Do not let any lumps form in the sauce. Add salt and pepper to taste. Add 2 tsp of any black sauce e.g. Worcestershire, A-1, 8 to 8 etc. etc. for flavouring. Stir, taste, and take off the heat.

Note.

The mixture can be put directly into the greased loaf pan without lining it with grease proof paper. I prefer to line it with the paper as it makes it easier to turn out. However, care should be taken so that there are no creases in the paper or else the mixture will tend to lodge in these creases and when turned out will leave rough edges or gaping vents. A non-stick loaf pan is also a good option.

BEEF CASSEROLE

1 kg. stewing or, rump steak cubed	1-2 tblsp. oil
4 large onions sliced	2-4 medium carrots sliced lengthwise
2-4 medium potatoes sliced	1-2 large cloves garlic chopped fine
1 green pepper sliced	1-2 tblsp. flour
1 beef bouillon cube crushed	1 pt. water
½ cup cider or, apple juice	1 cup orange juice
1 orange peel blanched and shredded	Salt and pepper to taste

Method

Brown meat in hot oil. Sauté onion, vegetables, garlic, and pepper. Place meat in an ovenproof greased casserole. Add the sautéed vegetables reserving a few strips of green pepper for garnishing. In the same pan where meat and vegetables were cooked add the flour, bouillon cube and water. Mix well and bring to boil stirring constantly so no lumps form. Add the cider, orange juice. Stir well and pour over the meat and vegetables. Sprinkle half the shredded orange peel on top and reserve the other half for garnishing. Add salt and pepper. Lightly stir all. Cover and cook in a very moderate to slow oven for about 1½-2 hours or till meat is done. Before serving garnish with remaining green pepper and orange peel that has been kept aside.

Variations:

The beef can be substituted by mutton, pork, or chicken. About ¼ cup of cooked or half cooked rice may also be added with the vegetables.

CRUSTY BEEF PIE

2 lbs. beef (any cut) cubed

Salt and pepper to taste

1 bay leaf

2 carrots peeled and sliced lengthwise

4-6 thin slices of ginger

2 medium tomatoes peeled and chopped

10 oz of beef stock or, 1 beef bouillon dissolved in 12 oz. water

2 tblsp. flour

1 tblsp. oil

3-4 small onions peeled and kept whole

2-3 potatoes cut in round slices

A handful of green peas (optional)

Method

Coat the meat pieces in a combination of flour, salt and pepper sifted together. Heat oil, fry meat pieces till brown. Transfer to a greased oven-proof casserole. Add the bay leaf and all the remaining vegetables and sauté for about 5 minutes. Add seasoning and the liquid. Let the whole come to boil. Pour over the meat in the casserole. Cover and cook in a low oven for about 2 hrs or till meat and vegetables are done.

<u>*Pie Crust*</u>:

8 oz. flour

1 oz. margarine and 1 oz. lard or, 2 oz. margarine/butter, and 2 oz. *vanaspati* (hydrogenated vegetable oil)

1 tsp. salt

Milk for mixing

Sift flour and salt together in a bowl. Rub in the fats till resembles breadcrumbs. Add the milk gradually to form a soft dough. Roll out to ¼" thickness.

Uncover casserole and spread pastry over the stew. Alternately cut pastry into small rounds like scones and gently arrange them over the casserole starting from the edge overlapping each other. Brush top of pastry with milk and return to a hot oven. Bake for 25 minutes or, till pastry is evenly browned.

Variation:

1. The flavouring of the stew can be varied according to the individual's taste.
2. Instead of beef this dish may also be made with mutton or chicken.
3. The piecrust can be substituted with cooked pasta which should be spread over the stew and returned to the oven for 10-15 minutes to achieve a golden crusty texture.
4. Alternately boiled, mashed and creamed (with milk and butter) potato can be arranged in dollops or evenly spread over the stew. Return to oven till golden brown.

BEEF AND GINGER RICE

500 gm. any cut beef cubed	1 tblsp. (less if salty) light soy sauce
2-3 tsp. sugar	$\frac{1}{4}$ tsp. cinnamon powder
3 tblsp. brandy or, sherry	1 beef bouillon cube
2 cups boiling water	2 tsp. corn flour
Salt and pepper to taste	A handful of beansprouts

Method

Combine all the above ingredients except bouillon, water, and corn flour. Marinate the beef cubes in this mixture for about an hour. Place beef with the marinade in an ovenproof casserole. Dissolve bouillon in boiling water and pour over meat. Cover and cook in a slow oven till meat is cooked. Mix corn flour with a little cold water and stir into the gravy to thicken. Cook for another 2-3 minutes. Add salt and pepper to taste. Sprinkle bean sprouts on top and gently stir to mix. Reserve a few sprouts for garnishing if desired.

Ginger Rice:

1 tblsp. peanut or sesame oil	1 small onion chopped
1 cup long grained cooked rice	1 tblsp. preserved ginger chopped

Heat oil. Fry onion till soft and changes colour. Toss the rice in and mix well. Add the ginger and toss all well together. Serve the casserole turned onto a platter surrounded by ginger rice. 2 tsp. ginger powder can be substituted for the preserve.

BEEF ROLLS

500 gm. beef fillet thinly sliced	2 tblsp. oil
1 beef bouillon	1 large onion sliced
1 bay leaf	1 large carrot sliced lengthwise
¾ cup water	1 tblsp. corn flour

(The bouillon and water may be substituted with beef stock or beef broth

Filling

2 tblsp. br4ead crumbs – freshly made	1 small onion minced
1 tsp. mixed herb	1 tsp. chopped parsley
1 tblsp. butter	1 egg
½ cup canned mushrooms – finely chopped	Salt and pepper to taste

Method

Mix all the ingredients for the filling. Gently pound the meat slices with the back of a wooden spoon. Put a little filling on each side and roll up tightly. Heat oil and fry the rolls gently till brown. Lay them side by side with the over lapping side tucked underneath in an ovenproof casserole. Combine the rest of the ingredients except corn flour. Bring to boil and then pour over the rolls in the casserole. Cover and cook in a medium oven or microwave till meat is tender. Mix corn flour with 2 tblsp. of cold water and stir into the casserole to thicken the gravy. Cook for another few minutes uncovered till the right consistency is reached.

Variation: ¼ cup of long grained, brown, or wild rice may be added with the gravy. Alternately rice macaroni may also be added. In this case increase the liquid by another ½ to 1 cup. The addition of corn flour may not be required.

CABBAGE DOLMAS

1 medium onion finely chopped	1 kg. ground beef
2 tblsp. cooked rice	Salt and pepper (preferably freshly ground) to taste
1 cup stock or, bouillon cube and warm water	1 medium cabbage
1 bay leaf	2 tblsp. tomato purée
1-2 tblsp. parsley chopped for garnishing	½ tsp. caraway seed
2 tblsp flour/corn flour	

Method

Mix onion, meat, rice and seasoning well. Moisten with 1-2 tsp stock. Separate the inner tender leaves of the cabbage and wash. Put them in a pan of hot water for a few minutes. Take leaves out, drain the water and dab dry with a tea cloth. Put a filling of the meat mixture on each leaf and roll up like a sausage. Roll the dolmas lightly in flour and place in an oven -proof casserole in layers with the seams at the bottom. Make sure they are packed tightly. Do not let the dolmas overlap on each other.

Mix stock, bay leaf, caraway seed and tomato purée and bring to boil. Pour over *dolmas* just enough to drown them. Cover and cook in a medium oven till done. There should not be too much liquid. Pour off excess liquid if any before placing in the oven. Thicken liquid with corn flour adding extra stock if necessary and serve as a sauce. Garnish *dolmas* with parsley before serving.

Variations:

1. Use grape leaves if available instead of cabbage leaves.
2. Roll the cabbage dolmas in beaten egg and breadcrumbs and shallow fry. Serve with a salad and mashed potatoes or tomato rice. In this variation omit the rice and the caraway seeds in the filling. Cook the meat in 1 tsp oil with the minced onion, 1 small, chopped capsicum, and a few strands of spring onions. Add 1 tsp Worcestershire sauce and 1 tsp ketchup (optional) for flavouring. Tomato purée can be used as a substitute for ketchup.

OSANG OSANG BEANS (INDONESIAN)

1 tblsp oil (preferably pea nut)	2 medium onions sliced
250 gm. green tender French beans cut on a slant in 1" length	1-2 fresh green chillis deseeded and cut on the slant
1 small bulb garlic thinly sliced	400 gm. beef fillet cut in thin slices
1 cup water (more or less)	1 bouillon cube
1 tblsp. soya sauce	A pinch of ajinomoto or, any other gourmet powder, or sugar

Method

Heat oil in a fry pan. Put in the onions and garlic followed by the green chillis. Stir fry for a couple of minutes. Add the beans and the beef slices. Stir for 2 more minutes. Add the water, bouillon cube, sauce and ajinomoto. Cook for a further 3-4 mins or till done. Do not overcook. Serve with steamed rice.

OVEN MEAT BALLS

1 kg. good steak (chuck, round, stewing etc.) mince

1½ cup breadcrumbs or 3 slices bread

¼ cup onion finely chopped or ground

2 eggs

Salt and pepper to taste

½ cup milk

Method

Combine all above ingredients. Mix thoroughly. Shape into 4 dozen balls (*koftas*) about 1" diameter. Place on a greased baking pan and brown in a moderate oven for 25-30 minutes or till done. Test by inserting a toothpick into the middle of the balls. These may be wrapped in foil and frozen. Serve with the following Barbecue sauce.

Barbecue Sauce:

½ cup ketchup

2 tblsp. butter or, margarine

2 tblsp. light molasses

1 tblsp. vinegar

2 tblsp. water

Salt to taste

Add meat balls and heat through. Alternately cool sauce, add the meatballs, put in an aluminium or any other container and freeze till required. The above sauce is sufficient only for 1 dozen meat balls.

Variation:

Mutton, lamb, or chicken can be substituted instead of beef. Soya granules may also be used for those who prefer vegetarian. In this case, soak the granules for 1 hour, squeeze out the water and continue as the meat recipe.

MEAT BALLS WITH FETTUCINE

2 thick slices bread (not too fresh)

1 small onion minced

Salt and freshly ground pepper to taste

2 tblsp. oil (olive oil preferable)

500 gm. ground beef

2 cloves garlic crushed (optional)

1-2 eggs

3-4 cups thick condensed tomato soup or, tomato sauce according to the recipe below

Method

Soak bread in water or milk for a few minutes till soft. Squeeze out liquid, mash and mix with the ground beef. Add the onion and garlic, seasonings, and egg. Mix well and put all through the food processor once. Shape into small balls (e.g. *koftas*) and brown in oil. Drain off excess oil and place in an oven proof dish. Prepare soup according to instructions. Pour the soup or the tomato sauce over the meat balls. Add sufficient water just to cover the meat balls. Gently stir the liquid. Cover and cook in a low oven for about 35-40 minutes or till done. Uncover and gently toss the fettucine in. Cover and return to the oven for another 5-10 minutes. Serve with any salad of your choice.

Tomato Sauce:

Heat 1 tblsp oil. Fry 2 medium chopped onions till soft but not brown. Add 2 tblsp tomato puree and mix well. Add ¼ tsp. ground thyme and 2½ cups water. Cook on low heat for about 20-25 minutes stirring frequently. Add salt and pepper according to taste.

SWEET & SOUR BALLS WITH LO-MEIN

500 gm. ground beef

2 tblsp. corn flour

Salt and freshly ground pepper to taste

¼ green capsicum finely chopped

3-4 tblsp. sesame or, ground nut oil for frying

1 medium onion chopped fine

1 egg

1 stalk spring onion finely chopped

1 tsp. light soy sauce

Method

Combine all the above ingredients and put through the food processor once. Shape into small balls as above. Brown in oil, drain and keep aside. Make a sweet and sour sauce according to the recipe below and drop the balls into the sauce and bring to the boil. Lower heat and simmer for 5 minutes. Place on a bed of Lo-Mein and serve with extra soy sauce, chilli sauce and chillis in vinegar.

Sweet & Sour Sauce:

2-4 tblsp. ketchup

2 tsp. brown sugar

Salt and freshly ground pepper to taste

1 bouillon cube (chicken or beef) diluted in

1½ cup water or, 2 cups stock

1-2 tblsp. corn flour for thickening

1-2 tblsp. dark soy sauce

1-2 tblsp. red vinegar

1-2 tblsp. pineapple juice

1½ cup water or, 2 cups stock

Combine all the above ingredients in a saucepan and bring to the boil. Lower heat and simmer for 5 minutes. When all mixed well, taste if any additional ingredient is to be added.

Lo-Mein:

1 tblsp. oil

1 large carrot

4-5 large mushrooms

1 medium sliced onion

4-5 tender French green beans

50 gm. bamboo shoots

1 small green capsicum

250 gm. cooked Chinese egg noodles   2 stalks spring onions

A pinch of ajinomoto   1-2 tblsp. light soy sauce

Cut green beans, carrot, spring onions and capsicum in slanting thin strips. Heat oil. Sauté onion till the colour changes Add the vegetables except the capsicum and the spring onions. Stir fry for a few minutes and then add the Chinese egg noodles. Toss all together to mix well. Just before taking off the heat add capsicum and spring onions. The vegetables should not become too soft and soggy. They should always be crunchy. When the dish is ready add soy sauce and ajinomoto. Mix well and serve.

MEAT BALLS IN CHEESE SAUCE

500 gm. ground beef

1 medium onion minced

½ tsp. oregano

4-6 tblsp. oil for frying

1 egg

1 tblsp. breadcrumbs

Salt and freshly ground pepper to taste

Method

Mix all the above ingredients except oil and put through the food processor to blend well. Shape into small meat balls and shallow fry brown in heated oil. Drain oil from the meat balls and place in an oven proof dish. Make a cheese sauce as below and pour over the meat balls. Sprinkle grated parmesan and breadcrumbs on top. Dot with small dollops of butter. Cover and cook in a med. low oven till done. Serve with mashed potatoes and a salad.

Cheese Sauce:

Mix 2 tblsp butter, 2 tblsp flour and a small, minced onion in a saucepan. Stir over very low heat for 1 min. Do not let it stick to the bottom or burn. Gradually pour in 1½ cups milk stirring continuously till thick and smooth. It should be of pouring consistency. Make sure no lumps form in the sauce. Add a dash of tabasco for that extra flavour.

MEAT BALLS IN WINE SAUCE

(This dish is best made with beef. However, mutton/lamb or chicken mince may be substituted.)

500 gm. beef (any cut) minced fine	2 tblsp. heaped breadcrumbs or, 2 medium slices bread soaked in warm milk just enough to cover
1 medium onion minced	1 tsp. fresh or dried basil minced
Salt and freshly ground pepper to taste	1 tsp. sweet paprika
½ tsp. lemon rind (optional)	3 tblsp. oil for frying meat balls
6-8 small whole potatoes (optional)	6-8 fresh or, canned mushrooms or more

Method

Mix all the above ingredients except the mushrooms and potatoes, if using. Shape into small balls like '*koftas*' and brown in the oil. Drain and lay in an ovenproof casserole without letting them overlap. Potatoes fried a golden brown should be added at this juncture. If using fresh mushrooms sauté them lightly in the remaining oil and lay them on top of the meat balls. Pour sauce over, cover and cook in a med. slow oven till done, about 45 minutes-1 hour.

Wine Sauce:

1 tblsp. oil	1 beef, chicken, or vegetable bouillon
1 cup any red wine	3 cups warm water
1 tblsp. flour	

Cook flour and oil on low heat for 2-3 minutes stirring constantly. Do not let it burn or form into lumps. Dilute the bouillon cube in the warm water and gradually stir into the roux till well blended. Now stir the wine in and let all come to the boil. This sauce needs to be stirred throughout the cooking time. It should be smooth and well mixed.

Serve with a pasta or rice salad. Creamed and mashed potatoes with sautéed mint peas also make good accompaniments.

MEAT BALLS IN TOMATO SAUCE WITH NOODLES

2 slices of bread at least 2 days old	500 gm. lean beef
1 onion	Salt and pepper to taste
3-4 tblsp. oil	12 oz. or more noodles
2 cups "Tomato Sauce" – recipe given below.	

Method

Soak bread in water just enough to cover for about 5 minutes. It should get nice and soggy. Squeeze out the water by pressing the bread between the palms or through a strainer. Place the beef, onion and the bread in the food processor and process to a fine mixture. Add seasoning and then form into meat balls – around 16 to 20 balls. Wet hands in cold water before making the balls in case too sticky. Fry the balls evenly all around till brown by turning them frequently with a slotted spoon or spatula. Drain excess oil on paper towels. Make the tomato sauce. Place the meat balls in the sauce and cook over medium heat till the sauce penetrates the meat balls. Cook the noodles as per instruction and then gently stir into the tomato meat balls. Serve hot with a green salad. Alternately the noodles can be served separately, or the meat balls can be placed at the centre of a flat dish surrounded with the noodles.

Tomato Sauce:

2 medium onions chopped fine	1 tblsp. oil
2 tblsp. heaped tomato paste	1 pt. water
A pinch of thyme	Salt and pepper to taste

Sauté onions in oil till transparent. Add the tomato paste and mix with the onions. Add the water, thyme, and seasoning. Let mixture come to a boil and then simmer on low heat for about 15-20 minutes.

Variations:

1. Instead of browning the meat balls on top of the stove place in a moderate oven or microwave by smearing them well with oil about 2 tblsp.

2. Place meat balls in a heat proof dish, pour the sauce over, cover and cook in a moderate oven for about 30 minutes or a little longer. They can also be cooked in the microwave for about 10-15 minutes.
3. Replace onions with 3-4 cloves or more chopped garlic in the food processor.
4. Cook all the sauce ingredients omitting the oil, in a saucepan and bring to boil. Lower heat and simmer for about 30-40 minutes.
5. Instead of onion, mix 1 tblsp. or less of ginger juice with all the other ingredients of the sauce before bringing it to the boil.
6. Use 1 tblsp of corn flour during the last minute of cooking if a thicker sauce is desired.
7. Finally, instead of making the tomato sauce use 1 large can of any tomato soup. Prepare the soup according to instructions before pouring over the meat balls. Use any flavouring like ginger juice, garlic powder etc. etc.

TERIYAKI BURGERS

250 gm. ground beef

1 tsp. garlic paste

1 tsp. ginger paste

2 tsp. light soy sauce

1 tblsp. honey or, 2 tsp. brown sugar

Salt to taste

½ tsp. black pepper ground (optional)

¼ cup (more or less) oil

Method

Mix all the above ingredients except oil together and knead well to blend. Form into flat burgher patties. Roll lightly in dry flour and rest for 10 –15 minutes. Heat oil and shallow fry till brown and cooked through.

Note. This recipe can be used as a marinade for any other meat, chicken, or fish before grilling. Just add 2 tsp. oil to the marinade

----

EASY BARBECUED HAMBURGERS

500 gm. ground beef	2 tblsp. lemon juice
4 tblsp. vinegar	1 cup ketchup
1 cup onion finely chopped	1 cup celery finely chopped
1 tblsp. dry mustard	1 tsp. salt or, to taste
1 tblsp. brown sugar	½ tsp. black pepper freshly ground

Method

Heat the meat without oil until it loses the raw red colour. Keep aside. Put all the rest of the ingredients in a saucepan and simmer stirring from time to time until the onions and celery turn transparent. Remove from heat and add the meat. Once again return to heat, stir to mix, and warm. Serve sandwiched between hot "hamburger" or "hot dog" rolls. Instead of sandwiching can also be served on top of halved rolls.

Variation:

Ground beef can be replaced with ground mutton or chicken or if preferred, cooked fish is a good alternative for those who would prefer a fish hamburger! 1 small green pepper de-seeded and thinly minced can be used with the fish for added flavour.

HAMBURGERS (II)

1 slice bread soaked in 2 tblsp. milk	250 gm. beef ground
1 large onion finely minced	2 tsp. hamburger sauce
1 tblsp. ketchup or, tomato purée (optional)	1 tsp. hamburger seasoning
1 tsp. curry powder for extra zest	Salt and pepper to taste
1 egg (optional)	2-4 tblsp. flour
¼ cup (more or less) oil	

Method

Strain the milk from the bread and discard. Crumble bread and mix with the ground beef with all the other ingredients except flour and oil. Run the mixture in the food processor for a fine texture. Form into 6 round patties. Dust with dry flour and shallow fry on medium heat till well browned and cooked through. Sandwich between split hamburger rolls and heat slightly under the grill or an oven toaster. Smear patties lightly with mustard and ketchup before serving. Serve the hamburgers with a salad of julienned cabbage, cucumber, lettuce tossed with a generous amount of mayonnaise. Alternately, top each patty with a slice of grilled pineapple and a slice of mild cheese.

Variation: The hamburgers can be served as gravy cutlets instead of being sandwiched between rolls.

Gravy:

Brown 1 small onion minced fine and 2 tsp flour in very little oil. Add 1 cup of beef stock, ¼ cup ketchup or tomato paste, salt & pepper to taste. Bring to the boil, lower heat and keep stirring till gravy begins to thicken. Pour over the patties and serve with creamed mashed potatoes OR spaghetti in a tomato based (flavoured with oregano or Italian seasoning) pasta sauce and any salad of choice.

HUNGARIAN GOULASH (I)

4 heaped tblsp. oil (butter or fat is preferable)

1 kg. beef cut in pieces

Water as required

8 large onions sliced

2 heaped tsp. Hungarian paprika

Method

Melt fat in a heavy bottomed pan. Fry onion till golden. Add the meat and fry till colour changed. Now add paprika, stir 1 minute. Pour just enough water to cook meat. Cook till meat is tender. This dish should be thick with just enough gravy. Serve with rice, macaroni, or mashed potato, and a green or tomato salad.

HUNGARIAN GOULASH (II)

2 big onions chopped	2 tblsp. of any fat or, cooking medium
½ tsp. heaped hot paprika	½ tsp. heaped sweet paprika
600 gm. beef cubed or, 300 gm. beef & 300 gm. pork	½ tsp. caraway seeds
½ tsp. marjoram	1-2 green chillis (optional)
1 large green pepper (optional)	Water as required
3 big potatoes cubed	1 large red tomato chopped or, 2 tsp. tomato purée

Salt to taste

Method

Gently fry the onions in the fat till a nice and yellow colour. Add the hot and sweet paprika, stir. Add the beef, salt, caraway seeds, marjoram and the chillis and green pepper if using. Add enough water to cook beef. If using a combination of beef and pork, then cook the beef for half an hour and then add the pork adding a little more water to cover and cook for another 1 hr. The meat may also be cooked in the pressure cooker following the same method as above − beef first and then pork. When the meat is done add the potatoes adding a little more water to cover and cook till they are done. The tomato or tomato purée may be added either with the meat or with the potatoes.

Variation:

Lamb can be substituted instead of beef and pork. In this case use a little more fatty meat and the ribs.

SIMPLE BEAF STEAK

<u>Per person</u>:

1 fillet steak ½" thick	1 tsp. Worcestershire sauce
½ tsp vinegar	½ tsp. A-1 or any other steak or black sauce
2 tsp. oil	Salt to taste
2 tblsp. hot water	1 tsp. corn flour or, plain white flour

Method

Combine all the ingredients except the steak. Marinate the steak in this mixture for about half an hour. Place steak with a little of the marinade in a thick bottomed or non-stick fry pan. Cook slowly for 3-4 minutes or as desired brushing with the marinade from time to time. Turn steaks over and cook the other side till done. Put the steak on a platter. Add the left-over marinade to the pan juices with 2 tblsp. hot water. Scrape the bottom and sides of the pan well and let all come to the boil. Lower heat and simmer for 2-3 minutes. Stir and mix well. If necessary, thicken with 1 tsp corn starch or flour. Stir and blend well so there ae no lumps. Pour over steak.

Alternately, scrape the bottom and the sides of the pan. Add the corn starch and brown. Now add the water and blend well by continuously stirring with a blender or wooden spoon. Bring to the boil and then simmer as above. There should be no lumps in the sauce. Add more salt and pepper if required.

BARBECUED OR GRILLED STEAK

4 large steaks

1 tblsp. honey

1 tsp. ground ginger

1 tblsp. red vinegar

2-4 tblsp. oil

2 tblsp. light soy sauce

¼ cup red wine

1 tsp. ground garlic

Salt and pepper to taste

Method

Mix all the ingredients except the steaks together. Pour over the steaks, cover, and let rest for several hours or overnight in the refrigerator. Barbecue or grill steaks on low heat the next day, using the marinade to baste from time to time.

Alternately place the steaks with the marinade in a flat preferably non-stick fry pan and cook the steaks on both sides till done and the liquid has dried up. If too dry add a dot of butter to each steak. Serve with grilled large mushrooms, French fries, and a green salad. If a smoky flavour is desired sprinkle 2-3 tsp. bottled smoke flavour to the steaks just before cooking. Initially cover steaks to cook for 10-15 minutes (or to the desired doneness) and then uncover to cook further and dry off the liquid.

Note:

Chicken steaks from the breast can also be cooked as above – barbecued, grilled or pan cooked.

SIMPLE PEPPER STEAK (I)

1 fillet steak ½" thick per person

1 tsp. A-1 or any other black or steak sauce

2 tsp. oil or, 1 tsp. oil and 1 tsp. butter

Salt to taste

1 tsp. Worcester sauce

1 tsp. vinegar

1 tsp. whole black pepper

Method

In a bowl combine all the sauces, vinegar, salt, and 1 tsp. oil. Stick the whole black peppers on the steak. Beat with a meat tenderizer or the back of a knife lightly to partially break up and embed the peppers into the steak. Pour the marinade over the steaks and leave for half an hour or longer (overnight is better). Brush a frying pan with the rest of the oil or butter. Place steak carefully with some of the marinade. Cook for 3-4 minutes or as desired. Turn over carefully and cook the other side adding a bit of the marinade if necessary. When ready turn onto a platter. Now add 1 tblsp. hot water to the pan juices and scrape the bottom and sides of the pan and stir. Add the left-over marinade and let all come to the boil. Lower heat and simmer for 2-3mins. Pour over the steak and serve.

PEPPER STEAK (II)

(This is a little richer and needs longer preparation time of 10 to 15 days. Fill half a jam jar or any other jar with whole black peppercorns. Pour vinegar to the top of the jar. Forget about it till the day of the requirement.)

Per Person:

1 fillet steak ½" thick	1 large tomato
2 tsp. vinegar from the jam jar	1 tsp. heaped soaked peppercorns only, ground fine
2 small red onions chopped	
Salt to taste	A good handful of parsley chopped fine
2 tsp. olive oil + 2 tsp. butter	Cognac for flambé

Method

On the day of the cooking soak the tomato in boiling water for a couple of minutes. Now peel off the skin. Add the vinegar to the ground pepper. Now, in a bowl put all the ingredients except the steak and mix well. Heat olive oil and butter together in a steak grill or fry pan – non-stick is preferable. Place the steak in the pan and cook for about 2-3 minutes or as desired. Now turn the steak over carefully. Put 1 tsp of the above mixture on top of the steak and cook till steak is done. Place steak on a platter. Now add the remaining of the above mixture in the fry pan and fry all well. Pour this on top of the steak. Pour warmed cognac over all and light.

Note

If steaks are to be well done, lower the heat and cook a little longer.

STEAK & KIDNEY GALANTINE

1 lb. beef or 2 beef fillets	½ lb. or 1 large beef kidney
Water as required	1-2 pkts. gelatine
3-4 eggs hard boiled and chopped or thinly sliced	2-4 tblsp. cheddar cheese crumbled
2-4 oz. spaghetti cooked (optional)	3 small tomatoes peeled, seeded and chopped
Salt and pepper to taste	

Method

Cook the beef and kidney with enough water till tender. Drain, chop or slice thinly and cool. Prepare the gelatine according to the instructions on the packet and let it cool. Line a mould with a layer of egg. Next place the beef and kidney evenly on top. Cover the meat with the rest of the eggs. Now put the cheese and then the tomatoes on top. If using spaghetti cover tomatoes with it. Pour the cooled gelatine seasoned with salt & pepper over all, making sure it reaches the bottom of the mould. Refrigerate to set. When ready unmould on a platter on a bed of lettuce (optional). Surround galantine with peeled and thinly sliced tomatoes and garnish the top and alternate slices of tomatoes with parsley.

Variation:

Mutton or chicken can be prepared the same way. If using mutton use 1 lb mutton and ½ lb mutton kidney. When using chicken replace the kidney with ½ lb chicken or pork sausages grilled and sliced. Sliced or chopped ham can also be used in place of sausages with the chicken.

OVEN BAKED OR PRESSURE-COOKED LEG OF BEEF

3 tblsp. oil	1 large onion sliced thinly
1 bay leaf	2-3 fat cloves of garlic crushed
Salt and freshly ground black pepper to taste	½ cup red wine, cider, or wine vinegar
2 tblsp. bacon fat (optional)	1 large carrot sliced lengthwise
1 kg. leg of beef cut in cubes	1 medium apple chopped
1 tblsp. orange peel sliced finely or grated	1¼ cup stock or bullion cube and water
1 tblsp. butter/margarine	1 tblsp. corn flour
1 tblsp. red currant or guava jelly	1 tblsp. pimiento chopped

Method

Mix oil, onion, bay leaf, garlic, salt, pepper and wine or substitute. Marinate beef in this mixture for several hours. Marinate in the morning if to be prepared in the evening. Alternately, marinate overnight if to be cooked in the morning.

Take meat out of the marinade and brown in bacon fat. Place in an oven proof dish or pressure cooker. Add carrot, orange peel, apple and stock or substitute to cover beef. Cover and cook in a low oven for approximately 2½ hours or pressure cook for 30 minutes.

Heat butter in the pan where the meat was browned. Add the corn flour and the strained liquid (after mashing all the ingredients in it) from the marinade. Keep stirring and bring to the boil. Add the jelly, pimiento, and seasoning. Stir well to mix. Pour over the meat once again. Cover and cook either in the pressure cooker for another 15-20 minutes or in the oven for approx. 1 hour. or till the meat is done. Serve with mashed potatoes or steamed, buttered rice and a mixture of steamed chopped carrots, French beans and green peas tossed in fresh minced parsley and if preferred butter. The steamed rice and vegetables with parsley and butter may be tossed together as one accompanying dish.

Variation: The bacon fat and the butter can be replaced with sunflower oil if preferred. The butter in the rice and vegetable accompaniment could be replaced with olive oil.

CHEESY VEAL ESCALOPES

4 veal escalopes	1-2 tblsp. flour sifted
Salt and pepper to taste	1-2 eggs lightly beaten
4-5 tblsp. (more or less) fine breadcrumbs	1 small onion finely chopped
4 tblsp. oil	2-3 cloves garlic crushed
4 large tomatoes peeled and chopped	2 slices lean bacon or, ham chopped fine
8 slices mozzarella cheese	1-2 tblsp. Parmesan cheese grated

Method

If the escalopes are too large cut them in half or quarters. Roll them in a mixture of flour, salt and pepper. Dip them in the lightly beaten egg and coat with breadcrumbs. Let stand for 15 minutes or more. Heat oil and brown escalopes on both sides. Drain the oil and lay half of them in an oven proof dish. Add the rest of the ingredients except the cheeses to the pan in which the escalopes were browned. Sauté for a few minutes and then add the remaining flour mixture, egg, and breadcrumbs if any. Pour this mixture over the escalopes in the casserole. Lay the mozzarella slices over the mixture. Cover the whole with the remaining escalopes. Sprinkle parmesan generously over all. Cover and cook in a low oven for 45 minutes to 1 hour. Serve with a salad of your choice.

Variations:

Instead of 2 layers 3 or 4 layers can be arranged repeating the sequences as above. The final layer should be escalopes with parmesan sprinkled over. In the unavailability of good veal substitute with beef fillet (undercut) slices which makes this dish equally appetising. Deboned chicken breasts slightly beaten can also be substituted.

STUFFED VEAL ESCALOPES OR BEEF FILLET SLICES

4 medium sized escalopes or, fillets ¼" thick

1 tsp. garlic powder (optional)

2 tsp. wine or red vinegar

2 tblsp. flour

1 egg

4-6 tblsp. oil

Salt and freshly ground pepper to taste

2 tsp. Worcestershire sauce

4 medium thin lean ham slices

4 medium slices mozzarella cheese

4 large mushrooms (preferably canned) sliced

2 tblsp. fresh milk

4 tblsp. (more or less) fine breadcrumbs

Method

Lightly beat the escalopes or fillet slices with the back of a wooden spoon or meat mallet to make them thin and double the size. Be careful not to tear the meat. Marinate the slices in a mixture of Worcestershire sauce, vinegar, garlic powder, salt, and pepper for ½ hour. to 1 hour. Drain slices from the marinade and spread them on a flat dish. Lay a slice of ham on only one half of each meat slice. Next put the mushroom slices (may be chopped if preferred). If using fresh mushrooms sauté them lightly in 1 tsp. oil. Cover all with mozzarella slices. Now fold the empty half of the escalope or fillet slices over the stuffing like an envelope. Seal the edges carefully with a mixture of flour and water or just lightly beat the edges with the back of a knife or wooden spoon. Dust both sides of each packet with flour. Dip in egg lightly beaten with milk and then roll in breadcrumbs.

Repeat the egg and breadcrumbs process a second time. Let them rest on a flat dish for ½ hour. Heat oil and slowly fry the escalopes/beef fillets brown on both sides over low heat. To test whether cooked, pierce a skewer gently in the middle of each packet avoiding the stuffing. It should be done when the meat is no longer red.

Serve with a combination of mashed potatoes - softened with a little olive oil and flavoured with salt, freshly ground pepper, and finely minced and sautéed fresh garlic or just garlic powder – and a tomato or green salad

Variations:

1. In the above recipe omit the stuffing completely. Just marinade the veal or fillet slices, beat lightly to spread and then dust with flour, dip in egg, roll in bread crumbs and fry crisp. Serve with the same accompaniments.

2. Either of the above 2 recipes can be substituted with de-boned chicken breasts.

3. The marinade can be varied by substituting Worcestershire sauce with soy sauce and adding 1 tsp freshly ground garlic paste or just garlic powder and 1 tsp freshly ground ginger paste.

SALTED BEEF

1 kg. silver side of beef whole	1½ tblsp. of salt
½ tsp. saltpetre	2 tblsp. jaggery or, brown sugar
5 cloves freshly ground	2 large lemons or, 4 large limes

Method

Prick the meat all over with a fork. Mix all the above ingredients and rub on meat making sure they penetrate well. Place in a glass, plastic, or stainless-steel bowl. Stick the lemons (after the juice has been extracted) on the meat. Cover lightly and leave in the refrigerator for 3 days. Turn the meat around every day and stick the lemons back on it. After 3 days throw the water away. Add fresh water and cook till tender. Cooking period can be reduced if cooked in a large pressure cooker. When done let it cool. Slice and serve as cold meat with any salad or sliced cold potatoes and vegetables or, hot with a sauce of your choice and potatoes and vegetables.

PRESSED BEEF TONGUE

1 beef tongue well scraped and washed

10 whole black peppers

2 star anise

1" piece ginger roughly chopped

Water as required

Method

Put whole tongue with the rest of the ingredients and sufficient water in the pressure cooker for about 45 minutes or more. Cool and press tongue from the wide top side with a little (about 1" above the tongue) of the water. Throw away all excess water. Cut tongue in slices for sandwiches and a cold fare with salads or in cubes for curries, casseroles, stews etc.

Can serve sliced tongue with the following sauce:

Sauce:

1 tsp. oil

2 beef bouillon cubes

Salt to taste

6-8 cloves garlic peeled

2 tblsp. Brandy

2 tsp. soy sauce

2 cups or more water

In oil fry garlic cloves. Add soy sauce and beef bouillon cubes. Mix all well. Next add. brandy and water. Bring all to boil. This sauce should be thin. Add or lessen any of the ingredients according to taste. Salt should also be added according to taste as some soy sauces can be very salty.

Variations:

For those who are not keen on beef tongue, goat or sheep tongue may be substituted. Cook in the same way as above. But believe me the beef tongue has the best result and is more tasty!!

SUDANESE TONGUE

Cook tongue as in "Pressed Beef Tongue" .and serve with the following sauce.

Sauce:

1 tblsp. oil	1 whole bulb garlic crushed
3 onions thinly sliced	2 beef bouillon cubes crumbled
1 kg. tomatoes peeled and chopped	1 tsp. heaped ground black pepper
Juice of 3 limes	Water if required

Method

In oil fry garlic and onion. Add bouillon cubes, tomatoes, black pepper, and the lime juice. Add water only if necessary. This sauce should be thick unlike the previous recipe.

Note:

The actual Sudanese recipe recommends ghee!!

PORK

ORIENTAL PORK CHOPS

4 lean pork chops	1-2 tblsp. light soy sauce
1 tsp. garlic juice	1 tsp. ginger juice
2 tsp. vinegar	½ tsp. brown sugar
Salt and pepper to taste	1-2 tblsp. oil, depending on the leanness of the chops
1 tsp. ajinomoto (monosodium glutamate or any gourmet powder)	1 tsp. corn flour (optional)
2-4 tblsp. hot water	

Method

Marinate the chops in all the above ingredients, except hot water and corn flour, for 2-3 hrs. Lay the chops in a large shallow pan so the chops do not overlap. Cook over moderate to low heat. Cook each side 15-20 minutes or till both sides are done and the chops are cooked and tender. Do not let the chops get too dry. Lay chops on a flat serving dish. Add 2-4 tblsp. of hot water to the pan juices scraping the sides and bottom. Let it come to the boil. Thicken with 1 tsp. corn flour if necessary. Pour over chops and serve. Vegetarian or mixed fried rice is a good accompaniment.

Variation:

Alternately the above chops may be cooked in a moderate oven or under the grill. When done scrape the pan juices by pouring hot water and then continue as above in a saucepan over moderate heat.

CHEESY PORK CHOPS

4 oz. grated any cooking cheese	1-2 tblsp. fine breadcrumbs
4 lean pork chops trimmed of any excess fat	2-3 tblsp. oil
1 tblsp. onion minced fine	500 gm. tomatoes peeled and chopped or 2-4 tblsp. tomato purée
1 tsp. garlic mince	Salt and pepper to taste

Method

Mix cheese with the breadcrumbs. Dust chops with salt & pepper and then brush both sides with a little oil. Roll chops in the cheese mixture till well coated. Warm oil over moderate heat and brown the onions till golden. Add the garlic. When it begins to brown add the chops and brown on both sides carefully. Try not to let the cheese mixture fall off. Add the tomatoes, cover, and cook over gentle heat till done. If using tomato puree add a cup of warm water. Cook till chops are done. Place on a flat serving dish surrounded by fluffy steamed rice and green peas. A green salad makes a good additional accompaniment.

Variation:

Alternately, after browning chops put in a casserole. Chops should not overlap. Place tomatoes or tomato puree and a cup of warm water over the chops. Cover and cook in a moderate oven till chops are done. Serve the fluffy steamed rice and peas separately along with the salad. This dish may also be microwaved which will take less time to cook (10-15 minutes) in power 5.

TASTY PORK CHOPS

4 lean pork chops

2-4 tsp. dry mustard

1 bouillon cube powdered

1 cup warm water

1-2 tblsp. lemon juice

1 tblsp. brown sugar

2-4 tsp. tomato purée

1 medium onion chopped

1 tblsp. Worcestershire sauce

Salt and pepper to taste

Method

Place chops in a wide, shallow ovenproof casserole. Cook in a moderately hot oven uncovered for about 20-25 minutes to seal the juices. (Pour off all excess fat from the chops). In the meantime, combine sugar, mustard, tomato purée, bouillon cube, and onion together. Add 1 cup water, stir well, and bring to the boil. Add the Worcestershire sauce, lemon juice, salt & pepper. Stir well. Pour sauce over the chops. Cover and cook in a moderate oven till chops are done about 45 minutes to 1 hour. Serve with baked potatoes and salad or creamed spinach or both.

Variation:

1. When chops are half done add ½ cup half cooked rice or 300 gm. boiled noodles (tagliatelle or fettucine). This dish becomes a meal by itself. With the rice, sliced par-boiled potatoes may also be added, in which case omit the baked potatoes. The latter could also be omitted if pasta is being added to the chops. Creamed spinach or/and salad can remain as accompaniments.

2. Brown 4 lean pork chops in their own fat. Trim the residue fat if any and place the chops in a casserole and make sure they do not overlap. Add 1 tblsp flour to the remaining fat in the pan where the chops were browned. Blend the flour well with the fat with a wooden spoon. Add 2 tblsp tomato puree, 1 bouillon cube crumbled and 1¼ cup warm water. Bring all to the boil stirring continuously. Pour sauce over the chops. Add 1 bay leaf. Chop and brown 1 very large onion. Sprinkle over chops in the casserole. Cover and cook in a moderately warm oven for 45 minutes to 1 hour or till the chops are done. Serve as above either with baked potatoes, rice or pasta and a salad

SWEET & SOUR PORK BALLS WITH PINEAPPLE

4 slices pineapple cut in small chunks

2-4 tblsp. almonds blanched and toasted

Pork Balls:

500 gm. pork mince

1 tblsp. corn flour

2 tblsp. onion finely chopped

1 egg

Salt and pepper to taste

2-4 tblsp. oil for browning pork balls

Sauce:

1 tblsp. oil

1 cup pineapple juice

1 tblsp soy sauce

3 tblsp. vinegar

6 tblsp. water

½ cup sugar

1 tblsp. corn starch/corn flour

Method

Mix all the ingredients for 'pork balls'. Form into balls the size of a table tennis ball. Brown in oil and drain on paper towels. Keep aside.

Make the sauce by cooking oil and pineapple juice slowly on low heat for a couple of minutes. Mix soy sauce, vinegar, water, and sugar in a bowl. Add to the pineapple and oil mixture. Cook until the juice is thick and clear. Keep stirring continuously. If sauce is too thin, then thicken with corn flour. This sauce may be prepared and kept in advance.

Add the pineapple, almonds, and meat balls to the sauce. Heat all together thoroughly. Serve with boiled rice or Chinese noodles with different vegetables or green peppers deseeded and cut lengthwise. The following vegetables can be used after cutting them in slices lengthwise and blanching them in boiling hot water for 1 min - cabbage, carrot, French bean, Chinese celery etc.

PORK BALLS SWEDISH STYLE

4 tblsp. breadcrumbs

2-3 tsp. salt & pepper or, to taste

500 gm. ground pork

2-4 tblsp. oil for frying

1-1½ cup milk

1 large onion minced

2 eggs

Method

Soak bread in milk for about 10 minutes. Add the salt, pepper and onions and leave for another 10 minutes. Now add the meat and eggs and stir for all to mix. Make into small balls (like *koftas*) and fry on medium low heat stirring continuously to brown evenly. Make sure the balls are cooked inside. Test by inserting a toothpick. Continue frying if it looks pink or red. Serve hot with mashed and creamed potatoes OR boiled, sliced potatoes sautéed in oil/butter and coated with finely chopped mint or parsley leaves AND a bowl of mixed steamed vegetables (peas, carrots etc.) with a dollop of melted butter and a sprinkling of any herb. A tomato or bread salad may also be thrown in as an additional accompaniment. Also serve chunks of brown bread to make it a perfect meal by itself.

SLICED PORK & NOODLES WITH PEANUT SAUCE

4-6 spring onions chopped	4 tblsp. extra virgin olive oil
4-6 tblsp. light soy sauce	1-2 tblsp. brown sugar
½-1 tsp. paprika or, a dash of any hot pepper sauce	¾-1 cup chunky peanut butter
1 kg. roast pork sliced or, fresh tenderloin cubed	275 gm. fettucine cooked
1-2 cups spinach chopped (optional)	¾-1 cup hot water

Method

Sauté the spring onions lightly in 2 tsp oil. Keep aside. Mix all the other ingredients except fettucine, pork and oil and bring to a boil in a saucepan. Add the slices of roast pork, fettucine, spinach, and the spring onions. Cook on low heat tossing gently for 1-2 minutes. Serve while still hot. The dish should have a thick sauce just coating the pasta, pork, and spinach. It should not be mushy.

Variation:

If using fresh pork marinate it in a mixture of 1 tblsp oil and ½ the soy sauce. In another bowl mix the peanut butter, sugar, paprika, salt & pepper, rest of the soy sauce, water and blend all well. Sauté the spring onions as above and keep aside. In the rest of the oil cook marinated pork till brown and tender stirring frequently. Add the peanut mixture and spinach tossing gently. Next add the fettucine and spring onions. Once again toss gently to coat the pork with all the ingredients as above. The dish should be of the same consistency as mentioned in the original recipe.

PORK WITH SAUERKRAT

4 tblsp. oil	2 tblsp. lean boneless pork cubed (approx. 1½")
1½ lbs. onions sliced	1 cup sour cream
1 large clove garlic minced	1 lb sauerkraut drained
1½ tsp black pepper ground	2 tsp, (or to taste) salt
2 tblsp. parsley chopped	1 tsp. thyme powder or dried
1 tblsp. dill leaves/coriander leaves chopped	1½ -2 tsp. caraway seeds
2½ cups beef broth or bouillon cube dissolved in 2½ cups warm water	3 medium potatoes peeled and quartered
1 tblsp. paprika	

Method

Heat the oil and brown pork. Remove when done, drain and keep aside. In the remaining oil sauté the onion for about 10 minutes stirring frequently. Add the sauerkraut and cook over med. heat for about 5 minutes stirring continuously. Add the browned pork along with all the rest of the ingredients except the potato, paprika and sour cream. Cover and cook on low heat for ¾ hour. Add the potatoes and continue cooking for about ¾ hour. or till the pork is tender. Stir in the paprika and sour cream and cook for another 5 minutes Serve with any thick bread.

SWEDISH CABBAGE DOLMAS

7 tender cabbage leaves

2 tblsp, rice

150-200 gm. pork ground

Oil for deep frying

½ cup water

1-2 cups of milk

Salt and pepper to taste

1 tsp. golden syrup

Method

Boil the cabbage leaves in salted water for a few minutes (do not over boil) Reserve the water and keep the leaves aside. Cook rice with a little water just enough to cover. The water shall be totally absorbed, and the rice shall be dry. Add the milk and cook like porridge till mushy. Cool. Add the pork, salt and pepper and mix well. Spread each cabbage leaf and place a portion of the pork filling on one side. Roll cabbage like a sausage or spring roll tucking in the sides to prevent filling from falling out. If necessary, tie with thread without knotting. Heat oil and deep fry brown. {½ butter and ½ oil or all butter may be used in place of all oil.} Pour golden syrup and cabbage stock over the rolls and cook on low heat for about ½-1 hour. Alternately place in a medium low oven or microwave low till done. Serve with the following sauce.

Sauce:

1 cup water

1 tblsp. flour

1 cup milk

Salt and pepper to taste

Mix all the above and cook over low heat till thick. The sauce should not form any lumps.

(Cabbage dolmas can be frozen for 2-3 months)

SWEET & SOUR PORK

1 tblsp. Chinese/Japanese wine or sherry or, 2 tsp. white wine and 2 tsp. sherry.

1 tblsp light soy sauce

1 egg lightly beaten with the soy and 3 tblsp flour

500 gm. pork loin/fillet cut in 1½" cubes

1 tblsp. corn flour or starch

250 gm. white onion cut in wedges

Oil for frying

3 green peppers (capsicums) seeded and quartered

250 gm. bamboo shoots cut in cubes

2 slice fresh or canned pineapples cut in wedges

250 gm. carrots cubed, and half cooked

Sauce:

6 tblsp. sugar

4 tblsp. soy sauce

1 tblsp. any white wine

2 tblsp. white vinegar

4 tblsp. ketchup or, 2 tblsp. tomato purée

1 tblsp. corn starch/flour mixed with ½ cup water

1-2 tblsp. syrup from the canned pineapple (if using)

Method

Mix the wine or sherry, soy sauce, beaten egg flour and corn flour. Coat the pork cubes well in this mixture. Heat oil and deep fry till crisp and golden brown. Drain on absorbent paper and keep warm in a low oven.

Mix all the ingredients (excluding the corn flour mixture) for the sauce in a bowl and keep aside. Heat 3 tblsp. {more or less} oil and fry all the vegetables for about 2 minutes together. Pour sauce over the vegetables. Cook till it starts to boil. Pour in the corn starch mixture and keep stirring till it begins to thicken. Add the fried pork and pineapple. Stir to mix well. Serve hot with Chinese fried rice or *Nasi Goreng*.

Note. All the vegetables and their quantity mentioned are optional. They can be increased, decreased, while some may also be omitted according to taste. All the items can be kept ready. Just before serving they should be heated and then assembled. The pork should be re heated to crispness in a hot oven.

OVEN FRIED PORK RIBS

3 tsp. salt or according to taste

¼ tsp. mustard paste

1¼ kg. pork spareribs (lean)

1 tblsp. butter

1 tblsp. light soy sauce

¼ tsp. white pepper

¼ tsp. fresh ginger ground or, ginger powder

1-2 cups of stock, water or 1-2 bouillon cubes softened in 1-2 cups water

Method

Mix salt, pepper, mustard, and ginger. Rub well into the spareribs on both sides. Melt the butter in an ovenproof dish large enough to hold all the ribs. Place the ribs over the butter face side down. Cook in a low oven for ½ hr. Pour off any excess fat and pour sufficient stock or substitute over the meat. Cook for another 1 hour or till meat is done. 5-10 minutes before removing the dish from the oven add soy sauce.

Serve with mashed and creamed potatoes and a green salad or a dish of any mixed vegetable (or both) of your choice enhanced with a little butter and parsley.

YAKINOKO OR JAPANESE BARBECUED PORK

3 tblsp. ground onion

2 tblsp. ground garlic

1-2 fresh green chillis de-seeded and minced (optional)

½ tsp. ajinomoto

2 tblsp. "miso" (bean paste)

2 tblsp. light Japanese soy sauce

1 pork fillet cut into thin slices for grilling

Method

Combine all the above ingredients except the fillet slices in a bowl. Marinate the fillet slices in it for about 1 hour. Grill meat over charcoal or under the grill. The first method is always better. However, if using a gas or electric grill, add a dash of good quality smoke oil to the marinade to get the smoky flavour.

TAN CHUN (CHINESE SLICED PANCAKES)

Fillings:

500 gm. pork	½ tsp. ajinomoto
½ tsp. sugar or to taste	½ tsp. salt or to taste
½ cup onions minced	1 tsp. ginger minced
1 tsp. soy sauce or to taste	1 tblsp. white wine
1 egg	

Pancakes:

2 eggs	1 tblsp. water
Oil as required	

Method

Make pancakes by beating the egg together. Add the water and mix well. Brush non-stick frying pan with oil. Pour sufficient mixture to make paper thin pancakes. Stack them and keep aside till all done.

Lay a cheese cloth or any other thin cloth on the worktable. Place the pancakes singly on the cloth. Make a paste with 2 tsp corn flour and ¼ cup water and spread over the pancakes. Put the filling on top. Roll pancakes from right to left like a cigar. Wrap cloth around pancakes and steam {can be put in a steamer directly} for about 20 minutes. Cut into slices and serve with soy sauce as a snack or during a main meal with other Chinese delicacies, chow mein, fried rice etc.

FILLED HAM ROLLS

1 lb. puff pastry (keep in the refrigerator till required)

Filling:

6 tblsp. onion chopped finely	1 tblsp. or less butter/oil for frying
300 gm. smoked ham cut in small squares	A pinch/ or to taste nutmeg powder
3 eggs slightly beaten	2 tblsp. parsley chopped
4 tblsp. brandy	1 tblsp. parmesan cheese (optional)
Salt to taste	

Method

Fry onions slightly in very little oil/butter. Do not brown. Add all the other filling ingredients and 2 eggs (except the cheese). Cook till egg is set. Add the cheese now, only if using.

Roll pastry very thin as quickly as possible. Cut in squares – approximately 6" all around. Place 1 tblsp. filling in the centre of each square and roll up like a cigar. Brush rolls with the extra beaten egg. Place on a baking tray or sheet which has been brushed with water but not greased. Bake in a hot oven for about 15 minutes till golden. Serve warm with a mixed salad.

Puff pastry can be substituted with ice box roll mix.

HAM, EGGS & TOMATO PIE

Short Crust Pastry:

1½ oz. margarine or butter	1 medium red tomato peeled and sliced
1½ oz. any vegetable shortening or fat	1 tsp. salt or to taste
6 oz. flour	Ice water

Filling:

1 large slice uncooked bacon (preferably collar) chopped into small pieces minus rind	1 medium red tomato peeled and sliced
1 tblsp. water & I tblsp. milk each	1 egg
Salt and pepper to taste	

Method

Mix margarine and shortening with flour previously sifted with salt, with 2 knives or wooden spoons till like bread - crumbs. Rest in the refrigerator till really cold to make pastry rise better. Next add ice water very gradually to make a firm dough. Place in the refrigerator again. Grease and flour a small shallow 6"-8" pie tin. Flour a pastry board and place half of the dough on it. Pat lightly with a rolling pin and then with the hands to get a fairly round shape. Roll out gently the shape and size required. Lift the pastry very gently on to the pie pan and smoothen out by patting and pulling it with the heel of the hand from the centre up to the sides. This is essential to ensure there are no air pockets underneath the pastry. Line the base of the pastry with the chopped bacon. Cover bacon with the tomato, which is for flavouring. Season egg and mix with the milk and water or all milk i.e. 2 tblsp milk. Beat all and pour over tomatoes and bacon. Cool for a while in the refrigerator.

Take out the second half of the pastry. Treat it like the first half. Cover pie with it. With a pair of kitchen scissors cut the extra bits hanging over the sides and seal the edges by pressing down with wet fingers. Take the extra bits of pastry and form into the shape of a flower and leaves and press down in the centre of the top pastry as a decoration. Make a few vents on the cover pastry to let the air out. During cooking these vents must be opened out 2-3 times or else the pastry will balloon out. Brush pastry with a little beaten egg or just plain milk to give it a glaze. Bake in a hot oven for ½ hr or till done. Cool and cut in wedges.

If a larger or smaller pie is required, the proportion for the pastry is always half the amount of shortening to the flour used.

STELLA MASHI'S SALTED PORK

4-6 boneless pork shoulder or leg
2 oz. saltpetre powdered
1 bottle pure vinegar

½-¾ kg. salt
2 oz. brown sugar
15-16 limes

Method

Place the pork whole without washing in a large earthen, ceramic, enamel, or stainless-steel bowl. Pierce the meat with a skewer and rub a portion of salt, saltpetre and sugar mixed together, into the meat. Next, take 5 limes and rub all over the meat squeezing the juice into it. Do not throw away the limes after squeezing out the juice. Stick them on the meat. During this process keep turning and piercing the joint so that the salt mixture and lime juice penetrate deep inside. This procedure should be followed twice a day (morning and evening) for 3 consecutive days. Similarly, divide the bottle of vinegar and pour over meat after each application of the above mixtures. Keep the meat covered in the refrigerator after rubbing with the salt mixture and juice each time. After the end of 3 days, let the meat rest in the bowl for another half a day without applying anything.

In a large saucepan bring enough water (to cover meat) to the boil. Put the meat without washing into the boiling water. Let this boil for about 5–10 minutes. Take the meat out and put it aside. Throw away the water. Wash the pan and again bring enough fresh water to the boil. Once more place the meat into it. Make sure the water covers the meat. Now keep cooking till the meat is tender. Take off heat. Carefully drain the meat and place on a rack to cool. Store in the refrigerator. Slice and serve when required. This can be added to salads or served on a bed of lettuce with other sliced vegetables as a cold platter accompanied with salads. This also makes great sandwiches. Very convenient to serve up in any form when unexpected guests drop in.

Before throwing away the second lot of water in which the meat has been cooked, take out the fat which forms on top. Drain all water from it and store in the refrigerator. This can be used in cooking any meat curry or in making "parathas" – Indian bread. However, in these days of cholesterol consciousness the above should not be habit forming!! However, for special gala occasions an exception could be made!!

Variation:

Beef makes an equally good cold dish. Use the same method as above but omit the vinegar. For cold beef the best cuts would be boneless meat from the shoulder, silverside/topside, rump, sirloin, chuck etc. Serving suggestions are the same as above.

GLOSSARY

Ajinomoto	Monosodium glutamate (MSG)
Aloo	Potato
Aubergine	Brinjal or egg plant
Ahrar dal	Yellow lentil. Also known as 'tuvar'
Au gratin	A dish quoted with sauce, sprinkled with cheese and crumbs browned in oven or under grill
Barfi, burfi	Dry and sugary Indian confectionary
Bati-charchari	Another type of dry Bengali curry
Beorek	A Middle Eastern pastry dish
Bhapa	Steamed Indian food
Brinjal	Eggplant or aubergine
Bhujia	Dry fried or oven roasted mixed savoury nuts, lentils etc.
Biryani (Biriani)	A special type of 'pilau' usually cooked with meat
Borgul	Cracked wheat
Bori	Shaped and sun-dried balls or lumps of lentils
Casserole	Slow cooked food in a covered heat-proof dish in oven or the utensil itself for such
Chanchra	Bengali dry curry of assorted vegetables
Chapatti	Or roti, handmade, usually round, flat unleavened bread
Charchari	Dry Bengali vegetarian curry
Channa	Cottage cheese similar to 'paneer'

Chenchki	Another type of Bengali dry vegetarian curry
Chop suey	"Mixed spice" in Chinese – an American dish of meat (chicken, beef, pork, prawn) cooked quickly with vegetables
Cholar dal	Lentil made out of split brown peas
Crepe	Word of French origin, fine pancake
Curry powder	A mixture of various Indian spices often used for making curries (commercially available)
Daab	Green coconut
Dal	Any Indian lentil usually with the specific type mentioned before e.g., moong dal
Dalia	Broken wheat used as porridge and in various other dishes
Dalna	Bengali curry with gravy
Dárazsfeszek	Sweet pastry of Hungarian origin
Doi	Yogurt
Dolma	Stuffed vegetable
Dum	Vegetable normally cooked under pressure
Eggplant	Aubergine, brinjal
Escalopes	Flattened meat or fish
Falafel	A Middle Eastern snack
Fettucine	A type of Italian flat pasta
Flambé	A dish, sprinkled with spirit, set alight before serving
Flan	An open tart filled with fruit, cream, custard etc
Galantine	French dish with meat or poultry served cold covered with aspic

Ghonto	A 'mushy' Bengali vegetarian (sometimes non vegetarian) curried dish
Granola	Cereal mixture made of many nutritious items
Gulab jamun	A very popular fried Indian sweet in syrup, brown in colour
Hilsa	Very popular migratory ocean fish caught in the rivers of Bengal delta, akin to 'shad' of the Americas
Hulwa	Also known as Hulva. Soft Indian sweet
Jackfruit	A tropical fruit eaten raw when ripe or cooked while green as a vegetable.
Jhaal	A Bengali curry with chilli hot gravy. Also, peppery or chilli hot
Jhole	Bengali stew
Kalia	A rich and spicy Bengali curry
Kalo Jam	Indian black berry growing in a large tree, supposed to have medicinal properties
Khasta	Indian flaky pastry
Kheer	Indian milk dessert
Kitchri	A mixed rice and lentil preparation
Kochuri	Indian snack of wheat casing and vegetable, lentil (sometimes meat) stuffing usually fried in round shapes
Kofta	Ground meat, fish, or vegetable ball
Korma	A type of rich meat/fish/vegetable curry
Langosh	Or 'Langosch; Hungarian savoury cake
Lo-mien	Chinese dish with noodles, vegetables, meat, shrimps, seafood, and wontons.

Ma	My mother-in-law, Nilima Ghosh, who had a small repertoire of some very tasty dishes.
Malai	Cream of milk
Malpoa	Bengali fried sweet pancake in syrup
Methi	Fenugreek
Meringue	Small pâtisserie made from egg white and sugar
Mishti	Bengali sweets in general
Moong	A green lentil
Moussaka	A meat and egg-plant preparation of Greek origin
Mousse	A cold souffle
Mowcha	Flower of banana plant eaten all over Southeast Asia and Bengal
Mummy	My mother, Ratnavali Baruah, who was a great cook and the daughter of Pragna Sundari Devi the writer of the ground-breaking cook book in Bengali
Pakhi	My sister, Lalitha Jauhar, from whom I learned some Punjabi dishes
Paneer	Another name for 'channa' or cottage cheese
Paratha	Handmade Indian shallow fried bread
Pulao	Also known as Pilau. A rich rice dish
Rasam	South Indian sour soup and eaten as a starter
Riki	My son, Dr. Richik Ghosh; a reasonably good cook, who developed a few dishes as a student, overseas.
Roti	Chapatti or handmade, usually round, flat unleavened bread.
Rosogolla	A Bengali cottage cheese ball in syrup

Saag	Leafy green vegetable e.g. spinach
Sauerkrat	Pickled cabbage of German origin
Sambhar	A South Indian spicy lentil preparation
Sandesh	A dry Bengali confectionary sweet made mainly with cottage cheese
Singara	A pyramid shaped savoury pastry (fried or baked) usually filled with curried items. Also known as 'samosa'.
Sara	My maid, who surprised us with some of her innovations in cooking
Sembe	Swahili word meaning coarse ground maize
Sorsé	Indian mustard or 'rape' seed
Stella mashi	My mother's friend, Stella Das, and a great cook.
Sukiyaki	A dish of Japanese origin
Sushi	Any fresh raw food dish – Japanese origin
Tarkari	A dry Bengali curry
Tengri	Leg or leg bone of animals (usually goats)
Teriyaki	A Japanese cooking technique where food is broiled or grilled in a special sweet soya sauce
Thore	Soft inside of the trunk of a banana plant – a popular vegetable of Bengal (rhymes with 'more')
Tortes	Open tart or rich cake type mixture baked in a pastry case
Zucchini	A vegetable also known as courgette

ALPHABETICAL LIST OF RECIPES

Recipe	Page
Aginares Á La Polita	17
Anchovy Roll	74
Apple Salad	43
Armenian Sheesh Kebab	160
Armenian Stuffed Cabbage	35
Baked "Lau" Or "Lauki" (White Gourd) With Cheese	24
Baked Chicken	124
Baked Crab	90
Baked Cubed Chicken Breasts	127
Baked Potato – Finnish Style	25
Baked Tomato Fish	57
Baked Zucchini	22
Banana Flower (Mowcha) Pizza Or Pie	27
Barbecued Or Grilled Steak	199
Bar-B-Q Whole Fish with Coconut Sauce	55
Bar-B-q'ed Or Grilled Chicken Tengri (Leg)	131
Battered Meat	165
Bean Curd	31
Beef And Ginger Rice	181
Beef Casserole	178
Beef Rolls	182
Beef'n Beans	176
Bengali Fish Chop	61
Black Pepper Chicken Fry	134
Braised Aubergine Or Cucumber	18
Bread Salad	37
Breaded Lamb Chops	154

Recipe	Page
Cabbage Dolmas	183
Cheese & Pineapple Hamburger	164
Cheesy Chicken With Sour Cream	114
Cheesy Pork Chops	214
Cheesy Veal Escalopes	204
Chicken & Asparagus	123
Chicken & Corn Bake (I)	121
Chicken & Corn Bake (II)	122
Chicken Baked With Garlic	125
Chicken Cognac	113
Chicken Fried In Cheese Batter	136
Chicken Muslim Style	141
Chicken Pancakes Au Gratin	128
Chicken With Oranges	105
Chicken With Sweet Hot Sauce	112
Chilli Chicken	138
Chinese Fish	82
Chinese Fried Chicken	137
Chola/Chana (Chickpea or Garbanzo Bean) Salad	45
Chopped Chicken Liver	142
Closed Lahmedjun (Armenian)	168
Cold Herring Swedish Style	95
Crab Casserole	88
Creamed Chicken And Noodle	143
Crepé A La Rognon	171
Crumb Fried Chicken Cutlets	133
Crusty Beef Pie	179
Curried Fish Cakes	63
Curried Orange Chicken	106
Curried Pasta Salad	48

Recipe	Page
Easy Barbecued Hamburgers	194
Filled Ham Rolls	225
Fish & Mushroom In Wine Sauce	72
Fish Brown Stew	91
Fish Chops - Economical	60
Fish In Black Bean Sauce	83
Fish In Garlic & Tomato Sauce	70
Fish In Oriental White Sauce	73
Fish Pie	54
Fish Roll	64
Fish White Stew	92
Fried Chicken A La Muslim	139
Fried Duck With Thick Spicy Gravy	148
Fried Prawns	96
Garlic & Chilli Prawn	86
Garlic & Lemon Carrots	10
German Farmer's Salad	42
Green Jackfruit Burgers	34
Green Papaya Salad	44
Grilled Chicken	130
Grilled Fish	51
Ground Beef & Baked Beans	175
Groundnut Stew	117
Guyanese Baked Fish in Wine	58
Guyanese Baked Fish Supreme	59
Ham, Eggs & Tomato Pie	226
Hamburger Cutlets	163
Hamburgers (II)	195

Recipe	**Page**
Hasselbacks – Swedish Baked Potato	23
Hungarian Fish (Rāc)	81
Hungarian Goulash (I)	196
Hungarian Goulash (II)	197
Indian Salad	46
Indian Summer Vegetables	16
Indian Summer Vegetables As Accompaniment	20
Italian Flavoured Baked Chicken	126
Karjalan Pirakat	26
Kashmiri Mutton Chops	158
Kowshwe	146
Lamb Casserole	156
Lamb Chops	153
Lamb Chops Casserole	155
Lemon Broccoli	12
Lemon Fish	78
Lemon Garlic Butter Fish	69
Lemon Green Papaya	13
Lemon Mint Carrots	11
Lobster In Wine Sauce	84
Malaysian Stuffed Fish	67
Malaysian Sweet & Sour Prawns Or Lobsters (Mesah Pedas)	85
Masala Or Spicy Pomfret	66
Meat Balls In Cheese Sauce	189
Meat Balls In Tomato Sauce With Noodles	191
Meat Balls In Wine Sauce	190

Recipe	Page
Meat Balls With Fettucine	186
Melezana (Greek Aubergine Salad)	41
Methi Aloo (Potatoes With Fenugreek Greens)	19
Mock Grilled Fish	53
Moussaka	169
Mowcha (Banana Flower) Kebab	33
Mummy's Duck Haari ('Cooking Pot') Kabab	149
Mummy's Masala (Or Spicy) Fish	100
Noky (Noodles) With Chicken Sauce – Czech Style	144
Oriental Pork Chops	213
Osang Osang Beans (Indonesian)	184
Oven Baked Or Pressure-Cooked Leg Of Beef	203
Oven Fried Pork Ribs	222
Oven Meat Balls	185
Pepper Steak (II)	201
Piquant Chicken	111
Piquant Chicken Stew	116
Pork Balls Swedish Style	217
Pork With Sauerkrat	219
Potato Chops With Roe Filling	76
Potato Pancakes In The Oven	30
Pressed Beef Tongue	208
Quick Chicken Stir Fry	135
Quick Spicy Chicken	109
Roe Pudding	77
Rudjak Genit – Indonesian Salad	40

Recipe	**Page**
Salted Beef	207
Sara's Egg Plant	15
Sara's Papaya Tarkari (Curried Green Papaya)	14
Saté Kambing – Indonesian Sheesh Kebab	159
Savoury Cake With Chicken Filling	119
Savoury Paneer (Cottage Cheese) Pie	29
Seafood Creole Style	80
Shami Kebab (I)	161
Shami Kebab (II)	162
Simple Baked Fish	56
Simple Beaf Steak	198
Simple Fried Spinach	9
Simple Pepper Steak (I)	200
Simple Tomato Salad	38
Sliced Pork & Noodles With Peanut Sauce	218
Smoked Hilsa - The Easy Way	94
Smothered Lobster Or Crayfish Meat	79
Spinach & Potato Salad	47
Spinach, Tomato & Cottage Cheese Pie	28
Steak & Kidney Galantine	202
Steamed Liver The Chinese Way	172
Stella Mashi's Salted Pork	228
Stellamashi's Hilsa Pārā (Pickled Hilsa)	93
Stewed Lamb Chops	157
Stuffed Crab	89
Stuffed Fish	102
Stuffed Roast Chicken	120
Stuffed Veal Escalopes Or Beef Fillet Slices	205
Sudanese Tongue	209
Swedish Cabbage Dolmas	220

Recipe	Page
Sweet & Sour Balls With Lo-Mein	187
Sweet & Sour Pork	221
Sweet & Sour Pork Balls With Pineapple	216
Sweet & Sour Prawn Balls	87
Swiss Chard Salad	36
Taboulé	39
Tan Chun (Chinese Sliced Pancakes)	224
Tangy Fish	68
Tasty Pork Chops	215
Tempura (I)	97
Tempura (Ii)	99
Teriyaki Burgers	193
Tomato Chicken	107
Tomato Eggs	32
Veal Loaf	177
Yakinoko Or Japanese Barbecued Pork	223
Yakitori – Chicken Sheesh Kebab Japanese Style	132
Youvourlakia Or Undressed Dolmas	166

www.ingramcontent.com/pod-product-compliance
Lightning Source LLC
LaVergne TN
LVHW061609070526
838199LV00078B/7225